OUIDA: A MEMOIR

OUIDA: A MEMOIR

BY

ELIZABETH LEE

T. FISHER UNWIN
LONDON: ADELPHI TERRACE
LEIPSIC: INSELSTRASSE 20

First Published in 1914

REMOTE STORAGE

PREFATORY NOTE

MY aim in writing this book has been to set forth a plain statement of the facts of Ouida's life and career. So many apocryphal stories had gathered round the woman and the novelist that it seemed desirable to clear the ground. As far as the material available admitted, I have allowed Ouida to tell her own story, and have intervened only when necessary to secure the clearness and coherence of the narrative.

The letters which appear in this volume prove Ouida to have been a woman of keen intelligence, marked ability, and indomitable spirit, and in any judgment we may pass on her we must never regard her only as a popular novelist. Ouida hated

> " All wrongdoing that is done
> Anywhere always underneath the sun " ;

and at a time when it was less common than it is to-day for a woman to descend into the public arena, and to plead for those who were down-trodden and oppressed, whether human beings or dumb animals, she never hesitated to espouse the cause of the suffering ; moreover, she had the courage of her opinions, although

5

they were rarely on the winning side. She advocated peace, justice to the peasant, and kindness to animals ; she deplored the desecration of the Tuscan country-side and the vandalism prevailing in Italian cities with almost Ruskinian eloquence. To-day, such views are held by most civilized men and women. In congratulating ourselves on these improved conditions, let us not forget to honour the pioneers.

Again, whatever be our estimate of Ouida's position and influence as a writer, it is clear that in assimilating and reproducing the spirit and charm of Italy as she does in her best novels, she deserves a high place among writers of fiction, and many who, following her, derive their success from the local colour of the scenes amid which the persons of their stories live and move, owe something to Ouida's initiative and skill. As a writer of short stories Ouida shows herself a true artist, and as a critic of books and men reveals independence of thought and judgment.

My information has been derived from many and various quarters, and I desire to express here most cordial thanks to all who have so kindly and readily rendered me assistance.

Special thanks are due to Mr. Fisher Unwin, with whom the idea of the memoir originated. After reading my article on Ouida in the second Supplement of the *Dictionary of National Biography*, he suggested to me to write a more extended biography. He has, in addition, given me valuable advice and assistance in

Prefatory Note

regard to the collecting of material, and permitted the printing of extracts from his own correspondence with Ouida.

I have also specially to thank Baron Tauchnitz for permission to print generous extracts from the letters [1] that passed between Ouida and his firm during the major period of her life,[2] and for his ready assistance in other ways during the preparation of the memoir.

To Mr. Montgomery Carmichael, British Consul at Leghorn, who by reason of his office came much into contact with Ouida during the latter years of her life, special thanks are likewise due both for information and for advice.

It is further my pleasant duty to offer sincere thanks to Ouida's relatives, connections, and early friends, Miss M. E. Mathias, Mrs. Francis Green, Miss Lockwood, Mrs. Charlotte Hunter, and Commander Claud Harding for information about the early life, and for the portrait of Mme. Ramé ; to Mrs. Callander of Ardinglas for information about Florentine society in the seventies and early eighties of last century, and for personal reminiscences of Ouida ; to Mr. Herbert Danyell-Tassinari (Herbert Dansey) for personal reminiscences, and for permission to print extracts from Ouida's correspondence with the Tassinari family and to reproduce Captain Danyell's drawings of the Villa

[1] Until 1892 the letters are addressed to his father ; after that date they are addressed to himself.
[2] 1865 to 1907.

Farinola and a drawing by Ouida[1]; to Mr. Lionel Robinson for personal reminiscences of Ouida in London and Florence; to Earl Curzon of Kedleston, the Right Hon. Sir Rennell Rodd, British Ambassador at Rome, Walburga, Lady Paget, Visconde George de Sarmento, Mr. Wilfrid Scawen Blunt, Mr. Sydney C. Cockerell, Director of the Fitzwilliam Museum, Cambridge, Mr. G. Milner-Gibson-Cullum, Vernon Lee, Countess Baldelli, Miss Millais, Mrs. H. C. Huntington, Mr. S. M. Ellis, Mr. Frederic Harrison, Mr. H. S. Salt, Mr. Henry James, Mr. Ralph Nevill, Mr. A. M. S. Methuen, Mr. Clement Shorter, Mr. G. K. Chesterton, Mr. A. L. Woodroffe, Miss Bella Duffy, Miss Maria Grant, Mrs. Fisher Unwin, Miss Julian Young, and Mrs. Conway Thornton for general information, or for permission to print letters and poems or to reproduce portraits and other illustrations.

ELIZABETH LEE.

KENSINGTON, *January*, 1914.

[1] See p. 115.

CONTENTS

ILLUSTRATIONS

I

CHILDHOOD AND
GIRLHOOD
1839—1857

OUIDA: A MEMOIR

CHAPTER I

CHILDHOOD AND GIRLHOOD
1839—1857

" THE Burg, Bury, or 'Berry,' as they call it, of
St. Edmund is still a prosperous brisk town ;
beautifully diversifying, with its clear brick houses,
ancient clean streets, twenty or fifteen thousand busy
souls, the general grassy face of Suffolk ; looking out
right pleasantly, from its hill-slope, towards the
rising sun : and on the eastern edge of it still runs,
long, black, and massive, a range of monastic ruins ;
into the wide internal spaces of which the stranger
is admitted on payment of one shilling. Internal
spaces laid out, at present, as a botanic garden. Here
stranger or townsman, sauntering at his leisure amid
these vast grim venerable ruins, may persuade himself
that an Abbey of St. Edmundsbury did once exist." [1]
So wrote Carlyle in 1843 of Bury St. Edmunds, a

---

[1] Cf. Carlyle, *Past and Present*, Book II, chap. ii.

town that has many claims to remembrance both for its historical and literary associations.

A monastery was founded there in the seventh century by King Sigebercht, the first Christian king of East Anglia, and to it was brought for burial, in the ninth century, the body of Edmund, the last king of East Anglia. But it was not until the eleventh century that the great building of "hewn stone" attained its full magnificence and importance. In 1214 it was the scene of the secret meeting convened by Stephen Langton, Archbishop of Canterbury, at which he read the articles that formed the foundation of the Great Charter to the assembled barons, who, after hearing them, took a solemn oath to exact a charter embodying them from King John.

In St. Mary's Church is the tomb of Mary Tudor, sister of Henry VIII, who married, first, Louis XII, King of France, and then Charles Brandon, Duke of Suffolk. John Lydgate, the poet, was a monk in the Benedictine monastery of Bury in the fourteenth century. Sir Thomas Hanmer, the editor of Shakespeare, H. W. Bunbury, the caricaturist, C. J. Blomfield, Bishop of London, and James Spedding, the biographer and critic of Bacon, were among those educated at the grammar school founded by Edward VI in 1550.[1]

---

[1] Bury St. Edmunds has also played its part in fiction. Charles Dickens makes it the scene of Mr. Pickwick's adventures at the ladies' school and praises it in *The Uncommercial Traveller* as "a handsome little town of thriving and cleanly appearance."

Childhood and Girlhood

It was in this town, with its romantic past and its pleasant surroundings, that the novelist to be known as Ouida first saw the light. She was born at 3.30 p.m. on January 1, 1839, at No. 1 Union Terrace,[1] the house of her grandmother, Mrs. Sutton. Her father, Louis Ramé, was a Frenchman who taught his native tongue in different schools in the town. He was a mysterious personage, and very little was known of him or his antecedents; he used to appear and disappear erratically, and where he went in the meantime no one knew. It would seem, indeed, that his wife's ignorance of his doings equalled that of outsiders, for in a diary kept by Mme. Ramé in 1866 she writes :—

"Had I ever known my husband's pursuits in any way and feigned ignorance of them, I should have been wrong indeed, but I did not, and even now it is only guesswork."

Ramé was a friend of Louis Napoleon during his exile in England, but quarrelled with him after the *coup d'état* of 1852. Ramé was much older than his wife and of unprepossessing appearance. But he had polished manners, was exceedingly clever, an admirable and witty talker, and a good whist player. It was supposed that he was connected with secret societies abroad, and that his frequent visits to the Continent and his sudden and unexpected entries and exits

---

[1] Now Hospital Road. The house has been named "Ouida," and a memorial tablet affixed to it is inscribed "Ouida Louisa de la Ramée, novelist."

were connected with those societies. On December 20, 1865, Mme. Ramé records in her diary :—

"This day recalls sad thoughts ; where now is the one whose birthday it is ?[1] Are my forebodings right that we shall never see him again? I wish my dear Louise could think with me on that point. True, he came so unexpectedly in '63 that there is no wonder she thinks he may come any day again. My own ideas are very different."

Ramé seems to have been fond of his wife's family, and to have been on good terms with them. Of one lady who possessed the kind of temperament that revels in woe, he used to say in his broken English, "She's never so 'appy as when she is mee-serable." He evidently had many English friends, for Mme. Ramé mentions a family in Devonport named Tolemarch whom her husband knew well, and relates the following story :—
"When one of the daughters ran away they sent for him to break the news to her father because he was so violent a man none of his family dare approach him. When M. Ramé went to tell him, all he said was : 'God bless my soul! I did not think the girl had so much spirit in her.'"

Ouida's mother, Susan Sutton, was the second of three sisters. Maria, the eldest, who was very pretty, married William Brown Lockwood. Lockwood belonged to a Suffolk family : his three brothers entered the Church and William was intended for the

[1] The last one spent together was in London in 1857.

same career, but falling in love with pretty Maria
Sutton, and the opportunity of entering a wine-
merchant's business coming his way, he seized it and
married, instead of waiting until he should have
obtained a curacy. His wife died in 1831, having
borne him three daughters—Maria, Henrietta, and
Fanny—and one son, William. Lockwood subse-
quently married his sister-in-law, Mary Anne, the
youngest Miss Sutton, who was also very pretty,
and had by her one daughter, Marianne. Lockwood died in 1839, but his widow survived until
1889.

Mme. Ramé named her daughter Maria Louise.
The godmothers were Maria Lockwood and Louisa
Le Neve (*née* Thacker), a schoolfellow and lifelong friend of Mme. Ramé. Mr. Le Neve died
within two years of the marriage, and his widow
married in 1840 Benjamin Harding, of Wadhurst
Castle, Sussex, where, in the forties, the Ramés paid
them several visits. It is to their son, Commander
Claud Harding, that this memoir is indebted for much
information about these early years. The little girl,
unable to pronounce the name Louise or Louisa,
called herself something that sounded like Ouida ; it
was Maria Lockwood who evolved the orthography
of the strange appellation, and Ouida became the name
by which the future novelist was known and the one
which she preferred to all others ; indeed, after she
became famous she used to be very angry if she was

described in any other way. In a letter to Baron Tauchnitz in 1882 she wrote :—

"The public has no business with what my name is or is not. Ouida is all they have a right to know."

Soon after she entered on her literary career, however, she styled herself Louise de la Ramé, and for some years signed herself so in her letters to friends.

In consequence of Ramé's erratic ways his wife had returned to her mother, Mrs. Sutton, at Bury St. Edmunds. Mme. Ramé had a little money of her own when she married, but her husband soon dissipated it. She also possessed a share in some family house property in Suffolk, which in 1866 she sold to the other participators. But there was never any formal separation between the husband and wife. During his absences Ramé was glad that his wife should have her mother's house to go to ; they remained on good terms, and Mme. Ramé had a great admiration for her husband up to his final disappearance. After the Commune of 1871 she never again heard of him, and it is supposed that he may have perished in the street fighting.

The marriage apparently brought Mme. Ramé little happiness beyond the child who was to be her lifelong companion, and to whom she was passionately devoted.

On the anniversary of her wedding day (January 16th) she writes in the diary for 1866 :—

Childhood and Girlhood

" A day of sad memory indeed, were it not for the one dear bright being who twelvemonths after gladdened my eyes and heart."

Later comes the entry :—

" Would I could make her believe with me that her poor papa has been wrongfully dealt with ; everything tends to confirm it."

The little girl was sent to local schools, but seems to have owed her chief education to her father. He talked to her on many subjects and inspired in her a love of history and mathematics. Every novelist, great or small, writes at least one autobiographical novel. In such a work fiction is certainly mingled with truth, but enough of the latter is there to be distinguishable. In 1878 Ouida published her novel *Friendship*. Etoile, the heroine, is, we know, intended to be herself, and Etoile says that her father, the Count d'Avesnes, a Belgian noble, " was a man of many ambitions, of no achievement. A political gamester, a political conspirator, his life was spent in the treacherous seas of political intrigue, and he at the last perished in their whirlpool. Little was known of him—by his daughter almost nothing. . . . Her father had come and gone, come and gone, as comets do. . . . He would kiss her carelessly, bid her do a problem or write a poem, stay a few days, and go. . . . He ceased to come. . . . His death was mysterious, like his life. He passed away and made no sign."

Ouida : a Memoir

We may certainly see here traits of M. Ramé.

Ouida was a clever and precocious child. A diary kept by her from April, 1850, to May 27, 1853, has lately been printed [1] in which she writes: " I must study, or I shall know nothing when I am a woman." She evidently read very much and very widely, for her novels contain references to and quotations from a large and varied number of writers in many tongues, that show acquaintance with early and modern literature. Some features of Ouida's own girlhood and upbringing are to be seen in those of Etoile, who " studied in the big books, and strayed about in the chestnut woods and orchards, and lived in her own fancies more than in anything around her. . . . The treasures of scholarship are sweet to all who open them. But they are perhaps sweetest of all to a girl that has been led both by habit and by nature to seek them. The soul of a girl whilst passions sleep, desires are unknown, and self-consciousness lies unawakened, can lose itself in the impersonal as no male student can. The mightiness and beauty of past ages become wonderful and all-sufficient to it, as they can never do to a youth beset by the stinging fires of impending manhood. The very element of faith and of imagination, hereafter its weakness, becomes the strength of the girl-scholar. The very abandonment of self, which later on will fling her to Sappho's death, or mure her in the cell of Héloïse, will make her find a cloudless

[1] Cf. H. C. Huntington, *Memories, Personages, People, Places* (1911).

Childhood and Girlhood

and all-absorbing happiness in the meditations of great minds, in the myths of heroic ages, in the delicate intricacies of language, and in the immeasurable majesties of thought."

Critics have over and over again ridiculed the inaccuracies in Ouida's allusions and references. Those inaccuracies cannot of course be defended, but the variety of her allusions testifies to the fact that at one time in her life books and reading played a great part. Most of her reading was probably done in early life, and she trusted later too much to her memory and did not verify her references.

The self-absorption which was to become one of her most marked characteristics was noticeable even in childhood, for sometimes at a children's party, instead of joining in the dancing and games, she would sit apart absorbed in a book. She invented for herself ingenious toys made of cardboard, representing a tournament, the little figures of men and horses being painted in gorgeous colours. She led a happy life with her cousins, the Lockwoods, and their friends, and many merry parties and picnics were enjoyed. There was no luxury, but at the same time no poverty, and the child grew up amid that middle-class life which is fast vanishing out of England, because it is either being absorbed in the artisan class, or, in its efforts to imitate the wealthier class, is losing the special characteristics that so long distinguished it.

In 1850 the little girl went with her mother to

Boulogne to join Ramé, and while there was taken to call on the Princess Letitia Bonaparte. Ouida was evidently fond of her father and regretted his many and lengthy absences. In 1851 she had an apparently light attack of smallpox : " I might have died, but, thank God! I recovered and without being pitted, which of course I don't care about so much as my life, but still I shouldn't have liked it," she observes in her childish diary. She paid a visit to the Great Exhibition of 1851. She took an interest in politics and public events even at this early age, and records an election at Bury—of which she makes use in one of her earliest published tales—the death and funeral of Wellington, and the proclamation of Louis Napoleon as Emperor, commenting that thereby the fickleness of the French nation was exemplified indeed : " France is no longer the greatest nation of the world." She was an ardent free-trader in those childish years.

Ouida had great affection and admiration for her godmother, Mrs. Harding, who again became a widow in 1849, when Wadhurst Castle was sold. In the early fifties she married Mr. Drane and went to live at Lee Lodge, near Lewisham. Ouida describes in her diary a visit paid to them there, and records with enthusiasm her feeling for her entertainers. " She is so beautiful and so amiable and kind ; I do love her so." The little girl calls her " the Queen " and quotes the line from Wordsworth, " a perfect woman nobly planned," in description of her. Mr. Drane, who was a very handsome and attractive man, she calls "the King." Writing in February, 1901, to Claud Harding on his mother's death, Ouida says :—

"I can never forget the adoration I had for her in childhood and the happy days at Lee Lodge."

Ouida's precocity showed itself in various ways. At the age of fourteen she wrote a history of England. At that age, too, she began to fall in love with any man who treated her with ordinary politeness, and imagined him to be equally in love with her. She made no secret of her sentiments, and even used to confide in "little Claud," then a boy of eight. No one would have been more surprised had they heard her confidences than the objects of her affection.

Ouida kept up a regular correspondence with Mrs. Drane for about thirty years, and hundreds of letters passed between them. Ouida's letters were very interesting ; and in them she gave her views of politics, society, and life generally with the greatest candour. Mrs. Drane told Ouida that she had left those letters to her son. She, however, begged that they might be destroyed, and as she expressed herself so very strongly on the subject, her wishes were carried out. When, on Mrs. Drane's death, her son informed Ouida that a legacy had been left her, she replied, ignoring the legacy, but asking to be assured that all her letters to his mother had been destroyed.

We have seen how, as a child, Ouida showed some

of the characteristics which later became so marked in her : her self-absorption, her capacity for imagining herself in love and others in love with her. Yet another characteristic may be included which was to play a large part both in her life and in her work— her love of nature and her love of beauty. Sometimes in her walks she would pick up a stone lying by the wayside, take it home, and make a sort of pet of it, saying it was lonely and uncared for. She acquired a considerable collection of such objects, all of which she endowed with the feelings of living beings. As she grew older she transferred such affection to dogs and horses, birds, and trees, and flowers.

Etoile, in whom we may always see Ouida, was brought up by her grandmother in a village on the Meuse, and the girl's love of nature is thus described :—

"She knew the whereabouts of every rare wild flower ; she knew every bird that haunted the woods or the streams ; she loved the wind and the wild weather as she loved the heat and the still moonshine when the nightingales sang in the orchards ; she was not dismayed if evening fell as she ran alone down a lone hill-side, or if she bore down through the swift wild rain like a little white boat through a surging sea ; she had the love of nature of a German and the unconsciousness that she loved it of a Greek."

Close to the house in which Ouida lived at Bury were the gates of Hardwick House, the property of

Childhood and Girlhood

Sir Thomas G. Cullum, Bart.[1]   The park and gardens are very beautiful, and there Ouida used to walk every day.   She is remembered as a lean, lanky girl in a crinoline, walking with her father.   From the windows of the drawing-room might be seen "emerald lawns, a giant copper-beech tree, and distant shrubberies; at the other end the window commanded a prospect of the northern terrace and the extensive meadows, where grazed the black and white cattle, which were so curiously marked that from a distance they appeared to be carrying white blankets across their backs for warmth."[2]

In her last years Ouida's thoughts turned to the haunts of her childhood, and in letters to Mr. G. Milner-Gibson-Cullum she constantly refers to the hawthorn-trees that are the glory of the park.   From Bagni di Lucca she writes in 1905 and 1906 :—

"Give my love to the blackbirds and hawthorns of your Hardwick. . . ."

"If I were you, when the hawthorns are out I should go to Hardwick and live in the trunk of a hollow tree. . . ."

[1] He died in 1855 and the baronetcy became extinct.   His grandson, G. Milner-Gibson-Cullum, who became a friend of Ouida in the later years of his life, succeeded to the property in 1878.

[2] Cf. George Vane, *The Love Dream* (1913).   (See *note*, p. 131.)

" If I had Hardwick I would live in a corner of it and never leave it. . . ."

" Tell the trees, the flowers, the birds, I do not forget the beauty of their home. Would it have been better with me if I had stayed near them ? Si jeunesse savait ! But, alas ! all that youth thinks of is to flee away into the sunrise light of what it believes to be the glory of the future. We are but unwise dreamers at our wisest." [1]

[1] The original of the letter from which the last passage is taken was presented by Mr. Milner-Gibson-Cullum to the Moyses Hall Museum, Bury St. Edmunds.

II

LIFE IN
LONDON
1857—1871

CHAPTER II

LIFE IN LONDON
1857–1871

IN 1857 Mme. Ramé with her mother, Mrs. Sutton, and her young daughter left Bury St. Edmunds for London. Ouida scarcely seems to have cherished much sentiment for her native town. When in 1907 it was decided to affix a tablet to the house in which she was born, she wrote to Mr. G. Milner-Gibson-Cullum :—

" This tomfoolery in Suffolk annoys me very much. I identify myself with my father's French race and blood, and I shall be greatly obliged if you would do your best to prevent any inscription of the kind you named being put as you say."

Yet a few days earlier she had in a letter to the same correspondent expressed a wish to go and see the old town if he would keep the secret of her identity. But consistency had little part in Ouida's character.

There is little doubt that M. Ramé's mysterious comings and goings scandalized Mme. Ramé's relatives and the society of a small provincial town ; the girl, who was certainly fond of her father, probably resented the criticism. And when she had left the town and had entered on her career as a novelist, her family doubtless assumed a more or less mid-Victorian attitude towards what for that time was the daring and outspokenness of her books. After she had become famous, her relatives, if passing through Florence, would call on her, and she would go to see them when she visited England if they chanced to be within easy distance, but she never again visited her native town. Suffolk plays no part in the various places in which Ouida lays the scenes of her novels and tales. The sole reference to it occurs in *Puck*.[1] The opening scenes are in Derbyshire, where the Lockwoods had gone to live, and Ouida would have acquired her knowledge of that district from visits paid to them. Here she introduces as a passing character a Suffolk agricultural labourer, who, in discussion with a Derbyshire miner, describes his native county of "Suffeck."

" 'Tis all butifull and flat as yor hand theer, none o't broke up into these nasty mounds o' yourn as is ony made to lame man and beast. Ye may walk hunderds of miles i' Suffeck, and hev it all as smooth and nice as a mawther's ap'on wi' the starch in."

He has also much to say about the conditions of labour, how in consequence of machinery "there's many more men than theer be things to dew. I'm better off nor most. I'd some schoolin when I was a brat;

[1] Published in 1870.

30

and I scraped—scraped till I got a cow, and I can make ends meet wi' the butter in summer-time. But there's a swarm o' men in the parish as dunno more'n their beasts in stye. Dunno their God; dunno their letters; never heard o' tha Queen, never put a mossel o' mutton in their mouths—dunno nothin'. Field-work is sickly-like, 'cos o' the wind and weather; and when yer comes to trampin' six mile out, and six in, and ditchin' and ploughin' all day i' the wet, it stan' to reason as how the rheumatic come hot and heavy arter a bit, wi' min and wimmin tew. Farmers, they kip their greyhounds t' run for cups and that loike; and kill sheep for 'em gainst their coursin-meetens; but their min they dew starve mostly; and the cupboard he's empty and the churchyard he's full. You see the lands is too small and min they're too many. That's wheer it be."

"Gentry take up sa much o't wi' woods for shootin'," grumbled the miner in answer. "If ye was ta til a' the groun' wheer's wood——"

"Nay, nay," objected the Suffolker. "That woan't dew. Woods is health to land; in field-work ye maun gie an' take, as wi' yer fellows. If you doan't gie timber elbow-room, yer soil 'll be parchin' wi' dry loike a duck in a hay-loft. If ye fell yer wood ivery wheers tha land she'll gape wi' cracks."

The Suffolker had never heard of emigration to new countries. Even Derbyshire to him is something very new indeed. "Ye're main and queer, wi' yer

31

land all muddled like into these ups and downs. Ye must ha' rare big moles to throw up such sky-high mouns." The last remark betrays the proverbial stupidity of the Suffolk yokel, for we are assured that it was uttered with no sense of humour, but in a very grave spirit of wonder and of inquiry. Ouida is here drawing on her early observation of the people among whom her girlhood was passed.

On coming to London Ouida, with her mother and grandmother, lived first at 41 Lansdowne Road, Kensington Park, and then at Bessborough House, Ravenscourt Park, Hammersmith. Dr. W. Francis Ainsworth, a cousin of W. Harrison Ainsworth the novelist, was their medical attendant, and to him the girl confided her attempts at writing stories. He introduced Ouida to Ainsworth, who was at that time editing *Bentley's Miscellany*. She submitted some of the stories to him ; he at once recognized their merit, and eagerly accepted them for his magazine. The first, entitled *Dashwood's Drag ; or, The Derby and What came of It*, appeared in the *Miscellany* for April and May, 1859, and she contributed stories to each succeeding number up to July, 1862 ; all of them were signed "Ouida."

The tales are vivacious and sprightly, and are remarkable for the knowledge displayed by a girl of twenty of such varied places as Norwich, Cambridge, Paris, a German *Bad*, Bohemia, Vienna, Scotland, Chamonix, most of which she had certainly at that time never seen. It is, however, this power of swiftly absorbing local colour from what she had heard or read, or from a very brief sojourn in the place in question, that is one of Ouida's greatest gifts. As she herself said later : "The supreme gift of the true artist is a rapidity of perception and comprehension." Her novel of *Pascarèl* (1873), the scene of which is laid in Florence and in the smaller towns and the country-side of Tuscany, is said to have been written after Ouida had only spent six weeks in Italy, and it remains one of the best descriptions of the kind we possess of that district.

Ouida's stories formed one of the chief attractions of the *Miscellany* in those years, and in the Epilogue for 1860 Ainsworth wrote :—

"We offer not our own opinion, but that of a host of critical commentators, when we say that few periodical writers have suddenly achieved a greater success than the contributor who has chosen the fanciful designation of Ouida ; whose sketches of society, both in England and on the Continent, are as graceful as they are accurate."

In 1867 fourteen of the tales were published in a volume entitled *Cecil Castlemaine's Gage and Other Novelettes*. One of the best of them is "Blue and Yellow," an election tale, the scene of which, Cantilborough, was probably Bury St. Edmunds, where Ouida had, as a child, witnessed an election. In the story she describes the place as "that clean, quiet, antiquated

town, that always puts me in mind of an old maid
dressed for a party; that slowest and dreariest of
boroughs, where the streets are as full of grass as an
acre of pasture land, and the inhabitants are driven
to ring their own door-bells lest they should rust
from disuse." The tale appeared in a French translation in the *Revue des Deux Mondes*, under Buloz's
editorship, in April, 1868.[1] It is introduced with a
few words of criticism in which Ouida is described
as "un écrivain dont l'exubérante imagination, la
verve facile, l'esprit courant, la désinvolture aristo-
cratique ont appelé l'attention du public anglais." It
should be noted that by 1868 Ouida had published
the long novels *Held in Bondage*, *Strathmore*, *Idalia*,
Chandos, and *Under Two Flags*. Among the con-
tributors to the numbers of the *Revue des Deux Mondes*
in which Ouida's stories appeared were George Sand,
the Comte d'Haussonville, Emile Burnouf, Paul
Janet, Emile de Laveleye and Emile Montégut. She
was thus in excellent company.

In January, 1861, Ouida's first long novel, *Granville
de Vigne, a Tale of the Day*, began to appear in *The
New Monthly Magazine*. It was concluded in June,
1863, when Tinsley published it in three volumes,
changing the title to *Held in Bondage* and paying the
author the sum of £50. Ouida was introduced to
Tinsley by Mr. Marsh, one of the principal managers

---

[1] Another of the stories, "Lady Tattersall," had appeared in the
same periodical in January, 1868.

for Chapman and Hall, who published *Bentley's Miscellany* for Ainsworth. *Strathmore* was begun in *The New Monthly Magazine* in the following month and ran until February, 1865 ; next month the first instalment of *Idalia* appeared, and was concluded in the number for February, 1867.[1]

Ouida was working hard in these years, and rapidly acquiring fame. In her mother's diary for the years 1865 and 1866 we find such entries as—

> *"October* 13, 1865.

"Went to New Burlington Street. Mr. George Bentley congratulated Louise very warmly upon the success of *Strathmore* and told her she must eventually take the highest position ; he spoke with great sincerity. We went also to Beaufort House ; there the printer told her how greatly it had sold.

> *" October* 26.

"Drove into Piccadilly with Louise to speak with Mr. Chapman about the publication of *Chandos*."

---

[1] These three romances were all written for Harrison Ainsworth, the proprietor of the two periodicals mentioned. It was at his suggestion that the original title of *Idalia* was changed, for he wrote to Ouida, on December 18, 1864 : "I do not like the title *The Lady of His Dreams*. It might do very well as the title of a poem, especially of the Tennysonian school, which I abominate, but it is too lackadaisical for a novel. If you can find nothing better, give it the name of the hero or heroine." The latter suggestion was adopted.

Ouida : a Memoir

On January 1, 1866, Mme. Ramé records that it is due to Ouida's exertions alone that they had a home such as they "have always had." A week later the entry runs :—

"I do try to economize as much as I can and pay as quickly. . . . Everything Louise earns is spent on the housekeeping, and except this one summer's trip to Clophill for a fortnight, not one year since our coming to London has she had change of air."

There are continual references to interviews with George Bentley and with Chapman, and also with Lippincott, who was responsible for the American publication of the novels, and who paid Ouida 200 dollars as her share of the sales of *Strathmore*.

News of Ouida's success had spread not only to France but also to Germany, and Baron Tauchnitz, when he visited London in the summer of 1865, called on Ouida with a view to including her novels in his well-known series. In October she offered him *Strathmore*, and in her letter mentions its success in England and America, "most triumphant," she writes, in the latter country, and in March, 1866, she offered *Chandos*, asserting "it is considered the most brilliant of my books." This was the beginning of Ouida's lifelong connection with the house of Tauchnitz ; she soon came to regard the Tauchnitz, father and son, not only as her publishers, but as her firm friends. A correspondence was begun with them which con-

FREIHERR VON TAUCHNITZ.

1816—1895.

To face p. 36.

tinued almost unbroken until 1907. While the correspondence throws light on Ouida's life and character, it testifies also to the unceasing kindness and consideration shown to her by Baron Tauchnitz and his son through that long series of years. From the beginning of the eighties until the close of her life, Ouida, through her reckless expenditure, her mismanagement, and her continual lawsuits, was always in want of money. She constantly asked Baron Tauchnitz for sums in advance for the work she was to deliver, often requesting that the money should be sent by return of post. To such requests a generous response was invariably made.

Considering, then, this long friendship, it will not be out of place here to say a word of the origin of the Tauchnitz collection of British authors. Christian Bernhard Tauchnitz, the founder of the firm, was born in 1816 at his father's estate of Schleinitz, near Naumburg. His uncle, Karl Tauchnitz (1761–1836), was the well-known publisher who issued the first collection of cheap editions of the Greek and Latin classics in Germany, and who first in Germany introduced stereotyped plates into his printing-works. In 1837 Christian founded the firm we know as "Bernhard Tauchnitz."

The chief undertaking of the firm, the collection of British authors, was started in 1841, the year in which the present head of the firm, Christian Carl Bernhard Freiherr von Tauchnitz, was born. Bulwer-

Lytton's *Pelham*, the first volume of the series, appeared
on September 1, 1841. At the present date the
collection comprises about 4,500 volumes ; every
work, from first to last, has been published by special
agreement with the author or his representatives. The
leading idea of the collection was the publication of
a continental edition of English works in the original
language, authorized by the writers, whose interests
were to be protected. In 1846 English works became
copyright on the Continent by literary treaties, but it
should be remembered that before that time they
enjoyed no protection. So, in a preliminary letter sent
to the most distinguished English authors, Tauchnitz
pointed out that he could embark on such an undertaking without the authors' permission, and that his
proposal to pay the English authors a sum for the
right of publication on the Continent arose from a
wish to make the first step towards a literary relationship between England and Germany. The proposal
found general acceptance on the conditions that an
honorarium should be paid to the author, that the
Tauchnitz edition should not be introduced into
England and the British Colonies, and that Tauchnitz
should have exclusive rights of publication for the
Continent. Tauchnitz at the same time undertook
not to hinder the sale of the original English edition
on the Continent. " I hope," he continued, " that
this first attempt to establish a connection with the
classical authors of England will lead to a long and

FREIHERR CHRISTIAN KARL BERNHARD VON TAUCHNITZ.

From a painting by Vilma ParLaghy.

To face p. 39.

advantageous relationship on both sides." That hope has been fully realized. As a general rule it was the author's popularity in his own country that secured the inclusion of his work in the Tauchnitz edition, but occasionally the merits of an English writer have been first recognized at Leipzig. When a book, like Du Maurier's *Trilby*, for example, was unusually successful, an addition was made to the honorarium originally paid.

In 1866 Freiherr von Tauchnitz took his eldest son, Christian Carl Bernhard, the present head of the firm, into partnership. He had spent a year and a half in England, and had come into touch with a number of the most distinguished English writers of the day, with many of whom his father was already on terms of close friendship. Among them were Dickens, Tennyson, Browning, Carlyle, Froude, Disraeli, Gladstone, Bulwer, George Eliot, Charles Reade, Kingsley, Wilkie Collins, and Trollope.[1]

The public were now becoming curious about Ouida's identity and personality; and gossip concerning her began to be spread abroad. In the early sixties it was a somewhat bold thing for three women to settle down alone in London without husband, son, or brother by way of protector, and for one of

[1] An interesting selection from the correspondence with those writers is printed in a little volume entitled *Der Verlag Bernhard Tauchnitz 1837–1912*, by Dr. Curt Otto, Tauchnitz's partner, privately published on the occasion of the seventy-fifth anniversary of the foundation of the firm.

them to earn a living by writing. A report got about that Ouida was divorced. "We want to know from whom!" writes Madame Ramé in her diary, and continues :—

"She is said to be Miss Evans, the author of *Adam Bede*, on whom great scandal rests—scandal to which I give little credence, knowing any about Louise or myself to be perfectly false ; therefore in all probability it may be so of her. Still, knowing that the highest in the land might be proud to call Louise their wife both from her talents and her virtues, it is hard to think vile and scandal-loving people should have power to injure her so as to prevent her being known as she ought to be."

But in spite of adverse gossip Ouida was gradually attaining a position of her own, and people, especially men, began to call on her—she was rarely throughout her life particularly gracious to women. Among these were Colonel Poulett Cameron, a distinguished Indian officer to whom she dedicated *Under Two Flags* in 1867, and Mr. Hamilton Hume, who, when her dog Beausire, to whom Ouida was greatly attached, died, made her a gift of a fine Newfoundland named Sulla. To Sulla Ouida dedicated, in 1870, her novel *Puck*, as "to a faithful friend and a gallant gentleman." People also discussed her books and hazarded conjectures as to the identity of her characters. She contradicted a report that Benoni in *Under Two Flags* was George Bentley.

Life in London

Ouida's love of animals, especially of dogs, which she preserved throughout her life, and which, despite her exaggeration of the sentiment, was eminently genuine and sincere, began early. Although Mme. Ramé shared her daughter's predilection for dumb animals, her love for them was occasionally tempered by the trouble the care of them entailed. Now and then Beausire kept them awake all night with barking and growling. Mme. Ramé makes the following reflections in her diary for 1866 :—

" No doubt the dog has his reasons, poor fellow, and wants us to understand him. I only wish I could do so, for of course one's sense tells one that no dog so intelligent would be so uncomfortable unless something to his canine sense influenced him. He is a beautiful creature and I am very fond of him, but it is sadly wearing when he is so restless, and I am sorry that ever Louise expressed a wish for a dog."

Ouida was photographed with this dog, and on his death, in March, 1866, her mother records :—

" Noble Beausire died. Both Louise and self fell ill after the dear dog's death."

Ouida was in the habit of carrying a portrait of her favourite dog in a locket worn round her neck. She would often detach it and hand it round for inspection, with the remark, " This is my hero."

The death of Mrs. Sutton, Ouida's grandmother, on September 22, 1866, in her ninety-fourth year, left Ouida and her mother more freedom. Mrs. Sutton was

41

buried in the family vault in the churchyard of Bury St. Edmunds. She was a very pretty old lady with silky white hair, a fair complexion, and blue eyes. Writing to Claud Harding many years after [1] from Italy, Ouida says :—

"I am glad you remember dear grandmama. What a lovely old lady she was!—and beautiful even in death. Save her, whom I loved dearly, all that early life has quite faded into a dream ; sometimes I cannot believe that I was ever out of Italy. It seems impossible."

The mother and daughter left Hammersmith, and for a time had no fixed address.

Ouida to Baron Tauchnitz.

"51 WELBECK STREET, CAVENDISH SQUARE
[*April*, 1867].

"*Idalia* is about to be dramatized here on the 22nd, with the loveliest of English actresses [2] in the rôle of Idalia. I do not go to Paris yet, as the accounts I hear are not very attractive of the Exhibition at present ; and I have so many friends to see with the London season. I have occupied fine apartments at the above address a fortnight, and find them more convenient."

A few days after the performance (April 26), Ouida wrote to Tauchnitz that it was "quite a triumph."

[1] About 1880.   [2] Miss Herbert.

Life in London

The " fine apartments " in Welbeck Street were soon inadequate for the young novelist's growing fame and social success, and she now, in 1867, began her custom, long continued, of staying at the Langham Hotel when in London. Here she gave parties, the guests at which were men, Lady Burton being the only exception, but Mme. Ramé was always present. Among the guests at different times were Sir Richard and Lady Burton ; Colonel Meadows Taylor, author of *Confessions of a Thug* ; Major Brackenbury, military correspondent of *The Times* ; Colonel Pemberton, who, as correspondent for the same newspaper, was killed in the Franco-Prussian War ; Whyte Melville, General Hamley, R. S. Escott, Bierstadt, the American landscape painter ; George Lawrence, the author of *Guy Livingstone*, by whose work Ouida's earlier novels were greatly influenced, and his *umbra*, H. Dering ; Hamilton Aidé, Mr. Lionel Robinson, Arthur A'Beckett, Lord Henry Lennox, Lionel Lawson (uncle of Lord Burnham), J. R. Planché, General Breckenridge (of the Confederate Army), Serjeant Ballantyne, Algernon Borthwick (afterwards Lord Glenesk), Sir Alexander Duff-Gordon, and Longfellow.

These parties had a purpose on Ouida's part beyond that of mere pleasurable social intercourse. She would set her guests talking on a subject about which she knew little or nothing, because she needed information on it for the novel she was writing or projecting. She was once asked how she knew so much of

43

life, and especially of men's lives. She replied, " I hear a sentence and that illuminates all." On one occasion she required to know something about duelling and introduced the subject by asking Hamilton Aidé what he knew about it. She either ignored or forgot the fact that his father was killed in Paris in a duel in 1830. But then, as throughout her life, Ouida cared little for any embarrassment her rudeness or odd ways, due often to her extraordinary absorption in herself, caused her interlocutors. On another occasion, when some young officers of the Guards were dining with her, and pipes and cigars were lighted, she said, " Now, gentlemen, suppose my mother and myself are out of the room. Smoke and drink as if you were at the club ; talk as if you were in the smoking-room there ; never think about us." [1] And they obeyed her to the letter.

In those days smoking in the presence of ladies was considered a serious breach of good manners, and any lady who permitted it was regarded, in the jargon of the time, as " fast." But although Ouida never smoked herself and was indeed throughout her life strangely conventional and unbohemian in her personal conduct, she could dispense with the ordinary conventions on occasion, and she not only wrote on the back of the menu card in French, " On est prié d'attendre et de fumer," but cigarettes were

[1] Cf. Tinsley, *Random Recollections*, i. (1900).

often smoked in the middle of dinner. Nearly all who assisted at these feasts in the late sixties and early seventies have passed away, and even were they still living it is unfortunately almost impossible to recapture good talk. Personality is the one thing that cannot be reproduced, and talk, if it be anything more than a string of anecdotes, can scarcely be separated from the personality of the speaker. But we may perhaps discover Ouida's views of dinners and dinner-table talk. There is a chapter in *Puck* entitled "His Views on Dinners," in which the dog discourses on the subject and doubtless expresses Ouida's own experiences and conclusions. After laying down the law that the guests should not number more than eight, that the menu should be short—"a dozen services are quite enough in all reason"—and that out-of-the-season delicacies should be dispensed with, the servants perfectly trained, the wines beyond reproach, that the host or hostess should have the supreme talent of selection, and also the supreme talent of leading the conversation unostentatiously but skilfully, Puck continues :—

" The one great element of success at a dinner is the talk ; and who shall give a recipe, as I say, for that ? It is a thing that goes by nature, like the gift of colour and of song.

" It is preposterous to say that your men do not talk well. I have heard talk to the full as brilliant and epigrammatic as anything the cleverest writer can put into

the mouths of his imaginary characters. When I hear
people protest that in real life no such witty converse
as you find in very witty novels can ever be met,
I wonder where these protestants have had the mis-
fortune to live.

"I think it is a mistake to think that tremendously
clever people are required to obtain radiant conversation. Your very great genius, your very abstruse
scholar, is often a very stupid fellow, so far as lingual
utterances go. The best men at a dinner are such men
as are to be found by the dozen at the best clubs in
London ; men of quick intelligence, of good culture,
of consummate worldly knowledge, and of just that
sparkling, mischievous, pleasant social wit which is to
conversation what the truffle is to cookery or the
champagne is amongst wines.

"Those men are to be found, and better companions
need never be sought. True, at some tables they may
sit silent, *morne*, and as contemptuous as their politeness permits, but, believe me, that is only because at
those tables you are boring them. Get them into a
congenial atmosphere, their tongues will go, their
mirth sparkle, and their laugh be heard as enjoyably
as any one can wish. They can be the most amusing
companions in the world ; if they are not so with you
it is your fault : you bore them in some way.

"Politics you should banish absolutely—if people are
not of one mind about them they are sure to quarrel
over them ; if they are of one mind no subject can be

drearier. Some little bit of political news, quite fresh from some Legation or some Secretary of State, before the world has heard it, is all that should be admissible.

" Any quite fresh scandal is a great relish ; especially if you know something about it that no one else knows. Perhaps you had better take heed that the chief of the actors involved are not present ; though, indeed, in this age you are all so entirely free from prejudice on these points that (if you be discussing a divorce, for instance) you need not mind the presence of the relatives in the least, scarcely of the husband nowadays ; the only person whose feelings must not be hurt is the co-respondent. Where this last interesting personage is in the plural you had better not invite two of them at the same time ; they are sure to have either too much jealousy or too much compassion for one another.

" *Du reste*—Don Juan is always a delightful fellow, and the most amusing guest you can ever obtain, unless, indeed, it be weighing on his mind that he will have to marry Julia Abbandonata. In which case, of course, you cannot expect him to be lively."

A good host, like a poet, is born not made, but a few precautions help to ensure the success of a party.

" In the first place, there is the care needful in the selection of your guests ; they must suit one another or you will have discord ; a mingling of classes or of opposite political parties is, I think, a mistake : men

are more at ease in their own caste ; if you introduce
an ' outsider,' he or she must be a very brilliant one.
. . . There is a certain unity of feeling, and common
likeness of tone and manner, in an order, still more so
in each ' set ' of that ' order,' which is, if made use of,
an essential aid to harmony in itself.   It is an infinite
ennui to a man to sit next to another who does not
catch his allusions flying ; it ruins conversation when
one person outside the pale fails to understand all that
is the cause for mirth or for chat within it.

" Likewise, you should be very careful not to let any
topic get worn threadbare ; the instant it is getting
the least bit of a bore, sweep it away with the brisk
besom of a fresh and welcome subject.

" A little scandal is, as I say, an excellent thing ;
nobody is ever brighter or happier of tongue than
when he is making mischief of his neighbour ; but it
is a two-edged sword that requires very dainty hand-
ling ; and all caps of slander unluckily fit so very
many heads that you must be heedful how you select
them.

" If it be a party of both sexes, ask people that are
a *little* in love with each other, for people a little in
love are always eager to shine ; but banish all *grandes
passions* ; they have an eloquence of their own indeed,
but they are very stupid society at a dinner-table.

" If you be a woman, DON'T THINK OF YOURSELF.
Let your heart and soul be with your guests, let your
whole mind be given to the guidance and the surveil-

lance of the conversation. Remember that your dinner is your campaign, and that on your skilful direction depends your victory.

"But then withal you must be quite at ease, not in the least preoccupied, or your influence will be *nil*; you must be always gay, alert, suave, ready to skim over a difficulty, to supply an hiatus, and to prevent a pause; you must lead with radiance and with tact, and yet you must be perfectly willing not to shine, and to let your powers lie *perdu* if your guests are in full career without you, and if your self-assertion would be their interruption."

Whether Ouida at her own parties at the Langham was actually the perfect hostess here described it is not possible to discover, but it is quite certain that she regarded herself as such, and it seems equally certain that the men who were present thoroughly enjoyed the evenings.

Ouida herself dined out in London a great deal in these years. In 1868 William Allingham met her at dinner, and described her in his diary[1] as "dressed in green silk, with a clever, sinister face, her hair down, small hands and feet, and a voice like a carving-knife." Her notion of her own importance is clear, since she told Mrs. Shirley Brooks,[2] on whom she

[1] Cf. H. Allingham and D. Radford, *William Allingham, a Diary* (1907).
[2] Cf. G. S. Layard, *Shirley Brooks: A Great 'Punch' Editor* (1907).

made a favourable impression, " As I talk better than others, I ought to be listened to even if singing is going on."

Besides a passion for dogs, Ouida at this time cherished a passion for Mario, the great tenor. When he made his appearance at Covent Garden, July 19, 1871, Ouida threw him a bouquet containing an ivory cigar-case, with these lines from Dante :—

> " Pietosi dissero gli Dei
> Oda la terra una volta la musica
> Del Ciel, e labbre toccaro di . . .
> Mario ! " [1]

She always had a large portrait of him in her room in her Florentine villa.

Ouida now assumed the position of a celebrity.

Ouida to Baron Tauchnitz.

" LANGHAM HOTEL,
" *June* 5, 1870.

" I am about to have a portrait painted by a celebrated artist, and this picture will then be engraved. . . . My reputation has very greatly increased since *Idalia* appeared."

There is a somewhat apocryphal story that after the

[1] " With indulgence—quoth the gods—let the earth hear for once the music of heaven. And they touched the lips of . . . Mario."

publication of *Idalia* her father chanced to meet her walking in Kensington Gardens. He stopped and warmly congratulated her on her success; she never saw him again.

In offering *Puck*, which had been published in May, 1870, to Tauchnitz, as "a perfectly fresh yet already famous novel," she told him "there has been quite a furore about it here." It was in process of translation in the *Revue des Deux Mondes* when the siege of Paris commenced.

Ouida always took the greatest interest in public affairs, and her letters throughout her life are full of comment, often very outspoken, on them and on those who guided them.

Ouida to Baron Tauchnitz.

"IMPERIAL HOTEL, TORQUAY,
"*September*, 1870.

"What marvellous events within the brief space since last I wrote you! You have cause indeed for triumph and my poor France for bitter repentance of the submission she gave to a corrupt and emasculated Government."

Ouida's sympathies, as will be seen later, were altogether with France, which she was in the habit of regarding as her native country.

She was now able to take holidays away from London. One summer she went to Hastings. While staying

51

at Torquay, in 1870, she was entertained by Bulwer-Lytton, who was living at Argyll House. Ouida was a conspicuous figure in the town, in a shiny sailor hat and a pilot coat, always accompanied by her big dog, who dragged her, a willing slave, up hill and down dale. On one occasion, indeed, the dog saved her from drowning. She had not perceived the incoming tide, and he called her attention to her peril by violent barking and frantic efforts to push her from the road she was so unwisely pursuing. The autumn of 1871 she spent at Brussels, where she acquired the local colour for her delightful story, *A Dog of Flanders*. She went on to Florence, where she spent the winter, and was so enchanted with the place that it became her settled home for the next twenty-three years.

Before entering on that period of her career it will be well to take a brief survey of the work she had so far accomplished.

By 1871 Ouida had published, besides the collected edition of her magazine stories, *Strathmore* (1865), *Chandos* (1866), *Under Two Flags* and *Idalia* (1867), *Tricotrin* (1869), *Puck* (1870), and *Folle-Farine* (1871).

The three first belong to the novels of society that Ouida never ceased to write throughout her career. The volume of stories issued in 1867 [1] had evoked a satirical article [2] contributed by Lord Strangford

---

[1] See p. 33.   [2] September 21, 1867.

to the *Pall Mall Gazette* that helped not a little to bring Ouida into notice. It opened thus :—

"This ought to be an invaluable performance, not so much from any intrinsic merits as from the light which it incidentally throws upon the author and upon English society. It is always interesting to see the first studies of great writers and artists, and so to mark the first germ of a thought that has afterwards formed the central idea of a masterpiece. The first rough programme, for example, which Milton prepared for *Paradise Lost* will always have a literary interest quite independent of its own merit. The slight stories which are collected in this volume by Ouida will have similar attractions for the students of future centuries. In them may be seen in their simplest form the elements which are afterwards combined to excite the wonder of the world. In her more elaborate fictions we may note several distinct flavours which are harmonized into a bewildering whole—the superhumanly beautiful woman who breaks hearts as coolly as crockery ; the delightfully wicked roué who ruins women by the score and shoots men by the dozen ; the horsy young lady with a turn for flirtation, and the sentimental cavalier after Sir Walter Scott, succeed each other in dazzling succession."

With a hit at Macaulay, the reviewer continued :—

"Perhaps, however, the book will be almost more valuable to the historian than to the critic of the future. The Macaulay of a few generations hence will find ready-made some of those truthful yet brilliant sketches in which his predecessor excelled."

The critic proceeds to draw a picture of society as if written by a future Macaulay who would use Ouida as one of his authorities :—

"'Of the young men of the nineteenth century,' he may say, 'we fortunately possess a portrait drawn by no common hand. Ouida—for by this mysterious name, which should perhaps be translated into our present dialect as Yessiree, did the great painter of manners describe herself—evidently moved in the highest circles of society.'"

And after quoting at some length descriptions taken from the stories, the article concludes :—

"If this be not a true picture of the English upper classes in the middle of the nineteenth century, it gives at least the ideal excellence to which the lower classes aspired."

As is often the case with a review of this kind, it created a demand for Ouida's novels and helped to ensure her vogue. A review of *Under Two Flags*, however, which appeared in the same journal a little later,[1] while mercilessly showing up its absurdities, praised several scenes as being in "a spirited style and rather more truthful and natural than usual." *Strathmore* and *Chandos* contain all Ouida's worst faults and extravagances ; but the desert scenes of *Under Two Flags*, notably Cigarette's desperate ride

[1] December 26, 1867.

to save the man she loved, are full of life, passion, and energy, and are written in a style that may almost be called restrained.

If the tradition did not everywhere confront us that Ouida wrote *Idalia* when she was sixteen, I should be inclined to say that it was inspired by Meredith's *Sandra Belloni*. But Idalia, who devotes herself and her beauty to the wresting of her country's liberties from its oppressors, is a purely imaginary type of woman, and lacks the reality and conviction of Meredith's heroine, and the hairbreadth 'scapes of herself and the hero are more startling than convincing or interesting. French critics consider that *Idalia* is inspired by the work of George Sand, with which Ouida was well acquainted. The book, however, contains germs of some of the qualities that were soon to distinguish Ouida's works. The scenery of the Carpathian Mountains is well described, and the setting is in harmony with the events that take place among them. The Bosphorus, Venice, and the Bay of Naples play a part in the story, and afford opportunity for fine descriptive passages. It is curious to note in a later novel—*Wanda*, published in 1883—a similar mountain setting, and a heroine who in some ways recalls Idalia.

Tricotrin marks a new departure. It is the first of the novels in which the heroine is a waif, a foundling, and the hero a wanderer, a man of genius, a musician, as here, or an actor, as in *Pascarèl*—always an artist who preferred a free life, unfettered by the conventionalities of civilization, to the fame and wealth and power that life in ordinary society would have brought him. "No wise man binds himself," Tricotrin says. "Though I am here to-day, I may be in the moon to-morrow. Life is a game of chance; so much the better. . . . The only man happy is the man who is free. And the only man free is the man who is at once philosopher and wanderer. 'Sans pays, sans prince, et sans loi!' His country, the world—his prince, his art—his law, his conscience and his choice." Ouida's work was becoming more and more known and appreciated in America, and *Tricotrin* is dedicated "To the American people, in cordial acknowledgment of their reception of my works, and to those men among them, both of North and South, whose characters I honour and whose friendship honours me." *Folle-Farine*, which appeared two years later, belongs to the same class of work; as in Tricotrin, the scene is France, the heroine is a foundling, a gipsy's daughter, but the hero this time is a sculptor, who only comes into his own by the Folle-Farine's sacrifice not of her life, but of her virtue. It is an advance on *Tricotrin*; it contains good dialogue, the tragic note is deeper, there is recognition of the inevitableness of things and of the continual struggle —a theme Ouida touches again and again—of the artist against a callous, unappreciative society.

In the novel entitled *Puck*, the tale is told by Puck,

a tiny Maltese terrier.   True, he is " only a dog," but a dog with an immensely good opinion of himself and of his powers of observation.   He has studied life ; he knows, or thinks he knows, everything about men, and more especially about women.   Puck has many adventures and goes through many vicissitudes : he relates what he sees, what he thinks, and much is to be learned from his conversations with the other dogs he meets. His conclusions, his philosophy of life, are set before us :—

"Of course, dogs think a great deal ; when people believe us asleep, nine times out of ten we are meditating. . . . Everything in creation thinks, that's my idea."

In all that Puck says we may certainly see Ouida's own views concerning the society she describes, which here again consists of fashionable folk of high degree, of the demi-monde and the stage.   Amid much that is false, meretricious, extravagant, and even ugly, there is a substratum of truth, and for the first time Ouida treats a theme that later, for personal reasons, came home to her—the cruelty of women to each other when they are rivals in love.

We must remember that much that now seems ridiculous to us in these novels of Ouida would have then been quite unperceived by the larger number of her readers.   At that time classes were more sharply divided : there was very little intercourse between ordinary middle-class people and wealthy members of the upper middle class, and none at all between them and the aristocratic class. The bulk of those who read these novels of Ouida were ordinary middle-class folk, and to them the doings described would have appeared quite probable and appropriate.

Signs of the vanity in the toils of which Ouida was held to the end of her days are not lacking in this first period of her literary and social career, but when we are inclined to censure her we should not ignore the extravagant praise bestowed on her by distinguished persons. Bulwer-Lytton wrote her an eight-page letter of praise on the publication of *Folle-Farine*, and Whyte Melville, after reading *Puck*, wrote to her as follows :—

" I have just finished *Puck* and congratulate you indeed. To my fancy it is far the best of yours, good as the others are. It has all their imagination and dramatic power, with a vein of the most beautiful sympathy and feeling running through it, and a true poetry in the descriptions that is entirely independent of language, although clothed in the most beautiful and appropriate words. It is quite a work even a *man* might cry over, and that one would read many times and like better each time. In short, I think it is a first-rate, first-class, first-flight novel."

Praise of this kind could not but feed the vanity of an inexperienced young woman.

III

FIRST YEARS
IN FLORENCE
1871—1878

CHAPTER III

"THE great white Seasons of the Santa Trinità rose like snow against the golden air. Monte Oliveto towered dark against the rosy glory of the west. There was a sweet sea wind blowing which fanned out as it went all the spiced odours of the pharmacies and all the scents of the budding woods. The shops of the goldsmiths, mosaic sellers, and alabaster workers gleamed and sparkled in the light. Everywhere there was some beauty, some fragrance, some treasure ; and above it all rose the wondrous shaft of the Campanile, glancing like gold and ivory in the sun.

" Where lies the secret spell of Florence ?—a spell that strengthens, and does not fade with time ?

" It is a strange, sweet, subtle charm that makes those who love her at all love her with a passionate, close-clinging faith in her as the fairest thing that men have ever builded where she lies amidst her lily-whitened meadows.

"Perhaps it is because her story is so old and her beauty is so young.

"The past is so close to you in Florence. You touch it at every step. Every line, every road, every gable, every tower, has some story of the past present in it. In the winding, dusky, irregular streets, with the outlines of their loggie and arcades and the glow of colour that fills their niches and galleries, the men who ' have gone before ' walk with you. The beauty of the past goes with you at every step in Florence. Everywhere there are flowers, and breaks of songs, and rills of laughter, and wonderful eyes that look as if they too, like their poets, had gazed into the heights of heaven and the depths of hell. And then you will pass out at the gates beyond the city walls, and all around you there will be a radiance and serenity of light that seems to throb in its intensity and yet is divinely restful, like the passion and the peace of love when it has all to adore and nothing to desire.

"The water will be broad and gold, and darkened here and there into shadows of porphyrine amber. Amidst the grey and green of the olive and acacia foliage there will arise the low, pale roofs and flat-topped towers of innumerable villages.

"Everywhere there will be a wonderful width of amethystine hills and mystical depths of seven-chorded light. Above, masses of rosy cloud will drift, like rose-leaves leaning on a summer wind. And, like a

magic girdle which has shut her out from all the curse
of age and death and man's oblivion, and given her a
youth and loveliness which will endure so long as
the earth itself endures, there will be the circle of the
mountains, purple, white, and golden, lying around
Florence."

Thus wrote Ouida in 1873 [1] of Florence, the city
in which she had settled two years earlier, and which
was to be her home until 1894.

In August, 1871, Ouida and her mother went to
Brussels, staying at the Hôtel de l'Europe. Excursions
were made into the Ardennes, and to the cities of
Belgium. The scene of the most charming of her dog
stories, *A Dog of Flanders*, published in 1872, is laid in
Antwerp and its neighbourhood, and there, as always,
she has seized the spirit of the locality and expressed
its characteristics with fidelity and charm. She reached
Florence in November, travelling through Germany
and the Tyrol,[2] and stayed first at the Hôtel d'Italie, and
then rented a furnished apartment for three months at
6 Via Garibaldi, Lung' Arno. "Florence is charming
just now and her climate quite perfect," she wrote to
Tauchnitz on November 10th.

Florence, "the beautiful small city set along its
shining waters, with all the grace of its classic descent,

---

[1] Cf. *Pascarèl*, chap. x.

[2] She wrote to Tauchnitz, November 3, 1871 :—
"I was delighted with the autumnal splendour of the German
forests as I passed through them into the Tyrol."

its repose of contemplative rest, its sanctity of imperishable greatness,"[1] had not yet sunk into a "little town of the provinces." For some years Ouida frequented its best society, which still retained much of its former brilliance, and the *salons* of Lady Orford, of Mme. Emilie de Tchiatcheff—a kinswoman of the Dalhousie family, married to a Russian—both of whom were Ouida's firm friends, of the Princess Anna Corsini, *née* Barberini, of the Marchesa Isabella Piccolletti, gathered all that was best in Florentine society. Youth, beauty, art, politics, the diplomatic world, were all represented at those houses. The author of a new play or a new poem, a new singer, invariably found his way to the Palazzo Piccolletti, just as any distinguished Englishman or Englishwoman would go to Lady Orford's. She was a very important personage. She received on Sundays after midnight. She was always attired in the fashion of thirty years before, and wore a sort of sacque-shaped jacket and a full round skirt that looked as if it missed its original companion, the crinoline. In the evening she discarded the jacket for an early-Victorian evening bodice which on gala occasions, was cut straight across from shoulder to shoulder. But, whether in morning or evening attire, she dredged her pale reddish hair with flour, evidently using the kitchen dredger in the process, scattering the flour impartially over her chignon and a huge heavy plait across her head, and over her shoulders,

[1] Cf. *In a Winter City*.

whether clad in velvet or satin or bared for the evening. She never wore any jewellery. She smoked, in the fashion known as "chain smoking," cigarette after cigarette of "Caporal" tobacco, rolling them one after the other, lighting the fresh one from the stump of the one she was throwing away, and very seldom using the evil-smelling sulphurous match of the country. In the evening a long rank Italian cigar with a straw in it was substituted for the cigarette. She used to drive about in an old shandrydan with all the stuffing showing through and foxes' brushes wobbling at the horses' ears to keep the flies off, and skins much the worse for wear stretched at her feet.

But, despite her oddities, she was in great request, and scarcely ever had an evening disengaged, and for all her strange dress and queer habits she always looked the great lady and had the beautiful manners of the old régime. She had a very caustic tongue, a fund of anecdote, and was the wittiest old lady imaginable. She had an amazing knowledge of everyone's family history, and was keenly interested in and had an astonishing grip of international politics. She was a prejudiced Tory, and could see no necessity for change of any sort, except in the marriage laws, her own matrimonial venture having been singularly unfortunate. She was a prolific letter-writer, and invariably wrote a long epistle in violet ink, signed "H. O." and scattered with pounce, when a couple of lines would have sufficed. She became a sincere friend to Ouida, who described her in her novel, *Friendship*, as Lady Cardiff in these terms [1] :—

"The Marchioness of Cardiff loved to call herself an old woman. But she had kept three things of youth in her—a fair skin, a frank laugh, and a fresh heart. She was a woman of the world to the tips of her fingers ; she had had a life of storm and a life of pleasure ; she turned night into day ; she thought no romance worth reading save Balzac's and Fielding's ; she did not mind how wicked you were if only you never were dull. She was majestic and still handsome, and looked like an empress when she put on her diamonds and sailed down a *salon*. On the other hand, she would laugh till she cried ; she would do an enormity of good and always conceal it ; she honoured unworldliness, when she saw it, though she regarded it as a kind of magnificent dementia ; and, with all her sharpness of sight, the veriest impostor that ever whined of his misery could woo tears to her eyes and money from her purse. She always wintered in Rome, and never lived with Lord Cardiff. He and she were both people who were delightful to everybody else, but not to each other. She was a Tory of the old school and a Legitimist of the first water ; she believed in Divine right, and never could see why the Reform Bill had been necessary. Nevertheless, Voltaire was

[1] Cf. *Friendship* (1878), chap. xii. The scene is laid in Rome, but Ouida is describing the Florentine society she knew.

her prophet and Rochefoucauld her breviary ; and though she saw no salvation outside the *Almanach de Gotha*, her quick wit almost drove her at times near the wind of Democracy. Anomalies are always amusing, and Lady Cardiff was one of the most amusing women in Europe."

Mme. de Tchiatcheff was another of Ouida's intimate friends. She was a charming woman and her *salon* was the rendezvous of most of the members of the Anglo-Italian community.

During these years, the winter in Florence was filled with a "joie de vivre," with a gaiety and "entrain" that afterwards departed from it. Certain fêtes and entertainments stand out, like the fancy-dress ball given by the Comte de Talleyrand, at which most of the Florentines present represented some distinguished ancestor or ancestress, and the famous hunt "Corso," when every one, men and women, wore red coats and which ended with a mammoth dinner-party at Doney's. One year half the town tore off to Milan to see Garibaldi make a progress through the city, one of his last public appearances. Queen Victoria, the Duke and Duchess of Teck, Prince Leopold—whom Ouida came to know fairly well and of whom she had a high opinion—were several times in Florence in the eighties. But curiously enough there was one side of Florentine society, the literary and artistic side, in which Ouida took no interest what-ever. Although she would put herself out of the

way to make the acquaintance of, and then to entertain
lavishly, some statesman or ambassador, or a member
of some great aristocratic family—but even these had
to be brought to her—such persons as John Sargent,
the painter, Maclean, the sculptor, Eugene Lee-
Hamilton, Vernon Lee, Mary Robinson, Paul Bourget,
all living in or frequently visiting Florence, she
entirely ignored. The acquaintance of these people
would have been of much service to her, but unfortunately in social matters she put worldly before
intellectual rank. Sometimes, it is true, the Duc de
Dino, a charming old man, and his nephew, Charles
Talleyrand, who was at one time ambassador at Berlin,
were to be seen at her house, but even for such
persons, whose friendship again would have been of
great advantage to her, she had not the necessary
patience.

It is probable that Ouida had only intended to
spend the winter of 1871–2 in Florence, but several
reasons determined her to settle there. The beauty
of the city and its surroundings and the delightful
climate appealed to her artistic sense ; her worldly
aspirations would be more easily realized since
Florentine society was less exclusive than that of
London, and, chief cause of all, perhaps, she had been
introduced on November 1st, 1871, to an Italian nobleman, the Marchese Lotteringhi Della Stufa, gentleman-
in-waiting to the King, and had conceived for him
the one great passion of her life.

First Years in Florence

Before finding a permanent home she lived at various addresses in Florence until, in 1874, she took the Villa Farinola at Scandicci, which she occupied until the end of 1888. She was writing busily during those early years in Florence between 1871 and 1874. Four short stories that had appeared in *Lippincott's Magazine* were published in a volume entitled *A Dog of Flanders and Other Stories* in 1872, and illustrated with four mediocre drawings by Enrico Mazzanti, of Florence.

Ouida to Baron Tauchnitz.

"FLORENCE
[*September*, 1872].

" The *Dog of Flanders* is causing great admiration, I hear, in England. Lord Lytton just writes me word how charming he finds them, 'full of such delicate grace of style.'"

One of the stories in the volume, "A Leaf in the Storm," dealt with an incident in the Franco-German War of 1870–71, and when it became a question of issuing it in the Tauchnitz edition, the Baron asked her to agree to omit the passage: " The soldiers[1] kicked aside the warm and quivering body. It was only a peasant killed ! " " My dearest Miss de la Ramé,"[2] he wrote, " we are not so barbarous as you

[1] The Uhlans.

[2] Ouida, soon after going to London, had expanded the name of Ramé into de la Ramé.

think." At the same time he admired the stories, in which he found "an irresistible charm of poetry," and desired to issue them. Ouida strongly objected to make the change and the following correspondence ensued.

Ouida to Baron Tauchnitz.

[FLORENCE,]
"*October* 12, 1872.

" I am very glad you esteem the stories so highly. It is generous in a German to feel so truly the pathos of tales which personally are antagonistic in many points to your country. Apropos of this, I should not like my English altered. . . . Surely a victorious nation can afford to endure adverse opinions? The severity with which the war was conducted was no doubt strictly politic and logical, and from a German point of view perhaps justifiable, but nothing can extenuate to the dispassionate observer many actions in it for which there was no military precedent—the burning of the villages and hanging of franc-tireurs were to me most inexcusable in any campaign, and I frankly own that the ending of the whole question in such an enormous financial fine is of heavy ill-omen to the future of the world. However, on those points you and I will always 'agree to differ,' and I promise faithfully not to weary you with any statement of these perverse views when I have the very great pleasure (I hope ere long) of welcoming you, my dear Baron, to Florence."

First Years in Florence

Baron Tauchnitz [1] *to Ouida.*

" LEIPZIG,
[*October*, 1872].

" I am sorry that you do not consent to make some alterations in ' A Leaf in the Storm ' ; the value of the tale would not diminish by it. But I am quite of your opinion : ' we agree to differ.' I detest with you the brutalities of war. They have been committed in every war ; they may have been committed in the last war on both parties, for vulgar passions cannot always be ruled. Therefore the responsibility rests on those who have so frivolously provoked the war, the French. If you were acquainted with the heavy sorrows, the deep afflictions, the heartrending scenes in German families caused by the war, your gifted pen would find much matter. Not all families have been so fortunately preserved as my own, though we had to go through great excitement. My two sons-in-law and my own youngest son were as officers with our troops, my son—officer in the Prussian Guards—severely wounded at Sedan. But God protected life and health of all three."

Ouida to Baron Tauchnitz.

" FLORENCE,
" *October* 26 [1872].

" A Teuton like you and a Latin like me can never possibly view the war in the same light either in its

---

[1] He always writes in English.

causes or effects. But this opinion need never, and I trust never will, interfere with the cordiality of our personal regard.

"Pray do not say the French nation wished the war. It was the effort of Olivier [1] and Napoleon to bolster up a waning dynasty; it was like all L.N.'s policy, a gambler's risk—he threw and lost—and, alas! the country pays the penalty."

Baron Tauchnitz to Ouida.

"Leipzig,
"*November* 5, 1872.

"There cannot be the least doubt that our differing opinions about Germany and France will—as to me—never touch our personal relations. In the contrary, I hope and wish that our cordiality will last for ever."

Ouida was now engaged on *Pascarèl*, the first of her novels that dealt with Italy. The scene is laid in Florence and the surrounding country. Incidentally, nearly every town in Tuscany is described, and the book still forms an admirable guide to the historical, literary, and artistic associations and the natural beauty of the district. It was published in 1873 in London and in the Tauchnitz collection. An Italian translation also appeared that year. Ouida told Tauchnitz that she thought it would be always in

[1] Ouida's spelling of proper names is not always impeccable.

demand on the Continent. Throughout her life Ouida persisted in believing that her books had a larger sale on the Continent than was actually the case, and so she fell into the habit of asking Tauchnitz for a larger honorarium. The fee paid her was gradually increased. Tauchnitz told her that so far [1] *Idalia* had been the most successful of her books. Unfortunately, no record is available of the sums she received at this period from her English publishers. Until the royalty system became general—a system she intensely disliked—she sold her copyrights outright. She said herself that £1,600 was the largest sum she ever received for a novel. But current report in Florence in the days of her greatest vogue—the seventies and early eighties—credited her with an income of £5,000 a year. However this may be, she assumed her own superiority as a novelist, and continually depreciated her contemporaries.

Ouida to Baron Tauchnitz.

[November 24, 1872.]

"What frightful trash English novel-literature has become! That *Simpleton* and *New Magdalen* are a disgrace to any men who know aught of the world. Those *Adventures of a Phaeton* ought to have been *very* pretty, but it has no plot and ends so stupidly. *Silk Attire* by that author contains the most egregious social blunders."

[1] This was in 1872.

Ouida : a Memoir

In January, 1873, she went to Rome for the first time, returning to Florence in March, and her appreciation of the Eternal City later found expression in *Ariadne*. She was now writing *Two Little Wooden Shoes*, and tells Tauchnitz that she was illustrating it herself. Ouida prided herself on her powers as a painter. Throughout her life she was accustomed to paint portraits of her friends, and adorned the walls of her rooms with them. She also drew and painted landscapes and flowers. But she had no talent whatever for such works. The portraits were caricatures —unconscious, of course, on her part—and those who looked on them found it difficult to refrain from laughter. She continually presented little paintings to her friends, who had to accept them with the best grace they could. For example, she made Mr. Henry James an *offrande* of a small painted panel, a view of a Lucca street. He characterizes it as "of a childishly primitive 'art' : really a child of seven or eight might have done it." Walburga, Lady Paget, who possessed many examples, presented them after Ouida's death to the Anti-Vivisection Society, the funds of which benefited by their sale.

Ariadne was published in 1874, and had, Ouida declared, "immense success all over Europe."

In 1874 Ouida took up her residence at the Villa Farinola. It was situated at Scandicci, about three miles from Florence. It was a grand old house, dating back to the eleventh century, standing high, sur-

VILLA FARINOLA.

From a pencil drawing by Arthur Danyell.

To face p. 74.

rounded by gardens commanding beautiful views. The country round it is some of the loveliest in Tuscany, "with winding roads under high hedges, gray old farm-houses hidden in olives and poplars, and fields going up hill and down dale, with the vines hanging everywhere, and the earth in spring-time yellow and scarlet with the multitudes of wild tulips."[1] The villa belonged to the Marchese Farinola, grandson of Gino Capponi.

Ouida had her own villa in mind when she wrote this description of an Italian villa in *Pascarèl* :—

"The villa was high up on the mountain side— vast, dusky, crumbling, desolate without, as all such places are, and within full of that nameless charm of freedom, space, antiquity, and stillness that does no less perpetually belong to them.

"Where these old villas stand on their pale olive slopes, those who are strange to them see only the peeling plaster, the discoloured stone, the desolate courts, the grass-grown flags, the broken statues, the straying vines, the look of loneliness and of decay.

"But those who know them well, love them and learn otherwise ; learn the infinite charm of those vast silent halls, of those endless echoing corridors and cloisters, of those wide wind-swept, sun-bathed chambers, of those shadowy loggie, where the rose glow of the oleander burns in the dimness of the arches ; of those immense windows wreathed with

[1] Cf. Edmund Yates, *Celebrities at Home*, first series (1877).

sculpture and filled with the glistening silver of olive woods, and mountain snows, and limitless horizons ; of those great breadths of sunlight, of those white wide courts, of those tangled gardens, of those breezy open doors, of those wild rose-trees climbing high about the Ætrurian torso, of those clear waters falling through acanthus leaves into their huge red conches ; of that sense of infinite freedom, of infinite solitude, of infinite light, and stillness, and calm. . . .

" It belonged to a great family, and the old chambers were still full of ancient and costly treasures."

Etoile's Villa Rocaldi in *Friendship*, although described in the novel as near Rome, is really the Villa Farinola. In a letter to Claud Harding, dated January 12, 1881, she wrote of the villa thus :—

"The villa is lovely inside and out. I wish I may show it you sometime. Across the woods and fields some four miles off lies Castagnolo ; beyond that Signa. I have a number of grand dogs, my horses are great pets, the place peoples itself with birds of all kinds."

The vestibule, decorated with palms, and plants, and the busts of the old Nerlé in niches in the walls, led into what was formerly a vast banqueting-hall but then a billiard-room. It was carried up the whole height of the building and surrounded by a gallery communicating with the rooms of the upper story. Out of it opened the ballroom, which looked on the upper garden. Choice prints of Bartolozzi and

VILLA FARINOLA : THE BILLIARD-ROOM.

From a pencil drawing by Arthur Danyell.

To face p. 76.

First Years in Florence

Smith hung on the walls, and lovely Turkey rugs were spread on the floor. On the left of the vestibule was a miniature-room, so called from the number of miniatures which decorated the walls, in which was displayed "objets d'art" of all kinds that Ouida had collected. She was an inveterate hunter of bric-à-brac, but had little real knowledge of it. Sometimes she chanced on a beautiful object, but sometimes got hold of mere rubbish. On the right of the vestibule was a room that Ouida made a winter working-room. Her writing-table was a beautiful and valuable one of Cinquecento work, oil paintings by herself hung on the walls, and her books, chiefly on art and history, found accommodation in this apartment, out of which opened the dining-room— a room that Ouida thought ought always to be one of the brightest in the house.

In summer Ouida worked in the ballroom, or garden-room as she called it. It was almost empty of furniture ; the large round table at which she wrote, an old ottoman sofa, an Italian stove, and a large portrait of Mario, and later of Stufa, formed its whole equipment.

The great glory of the villa was the garden, which Ouida has herself described for us in *Signa*.

" The delights of an Italian garden are countless. It is not like any other garden in the world. It is at once more formal and more wild, at once greener with more abundant youth and venerable

with more antique age. It has all Boccaccio between
its walls, all Petrarca in its leaves, all Raffaelle in
its skies. And then the sunshine that beggars words
and laughs at painters!—the boundless, intense,
delicious, heavenly light! What do other gardens
know of that, save in the orange-groves of Granada
and rose-thickets of Damascus?

"The old broken marble statues, whence the water
dripped and fed the water-lily; the great lemon-trees
in pots big enough to drown a boy, the golden globes
among their emerald leaves; the magnolias, like
trees cast in bronze, with all the spice of India in
their cups; the spires of ivory bells that the yuccas
put forth, like belfries for fairies; the oleanders, taller
than a man, red and white and blush colour; the
broad velvet leaves of the flowering rush; the dark,
majestic ilex oaks, that made the noon like twilight;
the countless graces of the vast family of acacias; the
high box hedges, sweet and pungent in the sun;
the stone ponds, where the goldfish slept through
the sultry day; the wilderness of carnations; the
huge roses, yellow, crimson, snow-white, and the
small noisette and the banksia with its million of
pink stars; myrtles in dense thickets, and camellias
like a wood of evergreens; cacti in all quaint shapes,
like fossils astonished to find themselves again alive;
high walls, vine-hung and topped by pines and
cypresses; low walls with crowds of geraniums on
their parapets, and the mountains and the fields beyond

them ; marble basins hidden in creepers where the frogs dozed all day long ; sounds of convent bells and of chapel chimes ; green lizards basking on the flags ; great sheds and granaries beautiful with the clematis and the wistaria and the rosy trumpets of the bignonia ; great wooden places cool and shady, with vast arched entrances, and scent of hay, and empty casks, and red earthen amphoræ, and little mice scudding on the floors, and a sundial painted on the wall, and a crucifix set above the weathercock, and through the huge unglazed windows sight of the green vines with the bullocks in the harvest carts beneath them, or of some hilly sunlit road with a mule-team coming down it, or of a blue high hill with its pine-trees black against the sky, and on its slopes the yellow corn and misty olive."

After the house and garden a great feature of the place was the dogs. Ouida adored them, and was always surrounded by a troop of them whom she fed and attended to herself. She was continually worried by people trying to sell her dogs. The peasants around her villa called her "la mamma dei cani." In a letter to a member of the Tassinari family she wrote :—

"You can't imagine the devices of your beloved Italians to get *soldi*. One man once implored me to take his puppy to save it. I told him I didn't want it, didn't wish for it, but he begged so hard and looked so miserable, I at last did take it and gave him some money out of pity. A year and a half afterwards he brought an action against me as owing him 30 francs for a dog! The funny thing was that the poor pup had died in the interim."

In a corner of the garden was a dogs' cemetery with costly monuments in marble and granite to her departed pets. It was so like a real graveyard that the Italians were shocked; they considered it irreligious and wasteful.

The beginning of Ouida's friendship with the Cavaliere Tassinari [1] and his family was due to a dog. A beautiful Newfoundland dog had been stolen from his villa of Sant' Ilario, near Lastra a Signa. He searched high and low for it and offered rewards, but without result. A year elapsed and the episode was almost forgotten, when one day Tassinari, passing by the Villa Farinola, was attracted by a dog barking at him over the wall. He recognized his own Newfoundland, and inquired who lived at the villa. He discovered it was Ouida, the famous novelist. He asked to see her and stated the facts. The evident joy of the dog at seeing him proved his case and Ouida acknowledged his right to the creature. She told him she had bought the dog from a contadino

[1] Cavaliere Giovanni Tassinari was in the Grand-Ducal days Grand Chamberlain to the Duke of Tuscany: he married a sister of Sir Edward Thornton, G.C.B. Tassinari's grandson, Herbert Danyell-Tassinari, has kindly allowed me to print extracts from Ouida's letters to his grandmother, and to his mother, Mrs. Danyell, and has himself given much valuable information.

VILLA FARINOLA : THE DOGS' CEMETERY.

From a pencil drawing by Arthur Danyell.

To face p. 80.

who said that it was his. Her mother had, however, become so deeply attached to Fido, as the dog had been re-christened, that Ouida begged Tassinari to leave it with her. She had spent a great deal of money on him, even taking a house in the hills for him during the summer months, so that he might not suffer from the great heat. Tassinari was touched by Ouida's evident distress at the idea of losing Fido, and as he had supplied his place by a boarhound, he promised to think the matter over. Next day Ouida, accompanied by Lady Orford, called on him and renewed her entreaties, describing her mother's distress when she heard the reasons of Tassinari's visit. Tassinari and his wife then gave up all claim to the dog, and so earned a title to Ouida's gratitude. A friendship ensued which lasted for many years and was of great advantage to Ouida.

As soon as she was settled in the villa, Ouida assumed all the airs and graces of a great lady, and showed all the caprices that are usually supposed to belong to genius. She set out to organize her existence in accordance with this estimation of herself and of what was due to so magnificent an abode.

It was a big place for Ouida to rent and keep up. A large regular income was necessary, and even then, if debt was to be avoided, prudence and business habits, which Ouida wholly lacked, would have been essential.

Besides the house servants and gardeners, a coachman and groom were required, for Ouida set up her carriage, and her little victoria lined with oyster-grey satin soon became very well known in Florence. It was drawn by chestnut ponies named Mascherino and Birichino, with bells and bunches of pheasants' feathers stuck in their harness. Later on she drove a pair of white ponies and the carriage was lined with white satin.

She dressed extravagantly, and in that way attracted attention, for to many she appeared plain and without charm, a fact she never seems to have realized ; indeed, she believed herself to be exactly like Etoile in *Friendship*. She was of medium height and had beautifully shaped, very small hands and feet, a characteristic of the Sutton family and one of which Ouida was inordinately proud. She always wore her sleeves and skirts short in order to display the one beauty she possessed. She had large blue eyes with a rapt expression. She wore her hair, which was "chestnut coloured, with a good deal of gold light on it,"[1] hanging down till she was long past middle age. She had her gowns made by Worth, the great Paris dressmaker of that period, and they were always of satin, fine cloth, or muslin. White was her favourite colour, but she sometimes wore pale blue or mouse-colour. Her shoes were of satin to match the gown, and she wore the same foot-gear in garden or meadow. She liked to receive guests dressed in white satin, seated

[1] Letter to Baron Tauchnitz, November 3, 1874.

in a red satin arm-chair, her feet stretched out to show their beautiful proportions. She usually made her mother dress in black by way of contrast. It is said of her by those who knew her at this period in Florence that she always dressed to fit the position of the heroine she was depicting at the time—white muslin if a peasant girl, white satin if a great lady. It was also her custom to reproduce in her books the clothes of the people she met.

Surrounded by her great white Maremma dogs, occupied with her books and her painting, she seemed to pass her life in a sort of novel of her own. She wove a web of romance round herself and her belongings, and only showed interest in those things and people that could in some way be woven into it.

"The first time I saw Ouida," writes the Countess Baldelli, "she was in her own apartment before an open fireplace, standing on a white bearskin dressed in a white flowing garment with wide open sleeves—in short, like a heroine of romance. Unfortunately, her physique did not correspond to its surroundings, and these only set off her disadvantages. Her voice, too, was monotonous, and I was disappointed. I expected a lively and interesting conversation and found her dull. There was a picture of a gentleman painted by her in the room. It was very like the person represented,[1] but looked more like a caricature, and a clever one, when to my surprise I found out

---

[1] Stufa.

the person represented was a dear friend and the picture meant to be a faithful portrait. . . . . She disappointed my expectations as a woman of talent."

Ouida instituted receptions on Mondays from three to six. Her coachman and groom acted as butler and footman. Her mother presided over the tea, which was served in the dining-room. It consisted of the worst Italian form of the beverage, served in cups of priceless Capo di Monte ; little cakes covered with pine kernels, a very cheap Italian delicacy ; and plates of the most expensive bonbons from Doney's, the famous confectioner in the Via Tornabuoni. For many years all Florence went out to see her on Monday afternoons, and every visitor of distinction of all nationalities attended these receptions. She could, however, be very rude, especially if she thought she was being made a show of, but was equally angry if her rooms were not filled. She never at any time encouraged casual visitors, and was invariably extremely annoyed if she was caught unprepared. She treated women, except her few intimate friends like Lady Orford, Mme. de Tchiatcheff, Lady Paget, Lady Windsor,[1] Mrs. Callander, Mrs. Danyell, with scant courtesy, and many anecdotes are told of her rudeness to them. On one occasion when M. and Mme. Waddington had accepted an invitation to tea, Mme. Waddington, as it happened, arrived before her husband, and before she could explain that he was following in another

[1] Now the Countess of Plymouth.

carriage, Ouida exclaimed, "Et M. Waddington—il ne vient donc pas," wholly indifferent to the presence of his wife.[1] Ouida and her mother, when the novelist was at the beginning of her career, once stayed for a short time in rooms at Clophill, near Ampthill, in Bedfordshire, where a connection of the family was curate. He gave an evening party for the distinguished authoress, whom many persons were anxious to meet. She arrived late, and on entering the porch of the little house was much disappointed to be shown in by a homely maid-servant. She evidently expected an ovation, and exclaimed in an indignant voice, loud enough to be heard in the drawing-room, "Where are your gentlemen? Is there no one to take my cloak?" Needless to say, this had a disconcerting effect on the few gentlemen present.

Among those who attended her Monday receptions were the Earl of Lytton, Lord Dufferin, Sir Augustus Lumley, Lord Savile, Lady Anne Chandos Pole, Lord and Lady Wolverton, and, indeed, all the distinguished residents in or visitors to Florence of every nationality. Ouida spoke both French and Italian fluently, but not by any means perfectly; she had, moreover, a deplorable accent, Italians not being always able to understand her.

Ouida rarely dined out in Florence on account of her delicate bronchial tubes, and when she did her hosts found

[1] Cf. *Italian Letters of a Diplomat's Wife* (1905).

her very difficult to deal with. If she met some one whom she did not desire to meet she would sulk the whole evening, and sometimes, even, would leave directly dinner was over. She had practised the same principles in London. Dining one evening at the Cashel Hoeys', Mr. Cashel Hoey took her in to dinner. Ouida began by asking him as a Civil Servant who were his acquaintances among the aristocracy. This was disconcerting to a modest official, and conversation became difficult. Ouida felt bored and insisted on going upstairs to the drawing-room before dinner ended. There she lay down on a sofa, rang for the servant, and asked if her carriage had come. It had not, and she remained silent on her sofa until its arrival. She was equally capricious in her likes and dislikes, and had none of the *savoir-faire* that enables persons accustomed to society to deal with an awkward moment.

These years were filled with her infatuation for the Marchese della Stufa. The story is a thorny one in the path of the biographer, and would be best ignored, were it not that the circumstance helped in determining Ouida to settle in Florence, and produced a lasting effect on her mind and art. She herself showed little reticence on the subject ; she talked and wrote openly of her feelings in the matter to her intimate friends, and declared that everything in her novel *Friendship*, which is based on the affair, was true, and the Florentines knew quite well for whom the characters were intended. It is probably a case where "everything is true and nothing is exact," to quote Maurice Barrès' rendering of Goethe's phrase : *Wahrheit und Dichtung*. It is sufficient to state here that Etoile is Ouida herself, and Prince Ioris, Stufa. After the publication of that book in 1878, Ouida's light in Florence from the social point of view waned, though certain of her friends stood staunchly by her. But the larger number resented the implied meaning of the book and withdrew from her the light of their countenance.

That she was passionately and sincerely attached to Stufa there is no manner of doubt, nor that she genuinely believed he intended to make her his wife. We have no means of discovering what his feelings towards her actually were. He was unmarried, but it is probable that a connection of old standing formed a bar to matrimony on his part. Some of his friends averred that he never meant anything serious in regard to Ouida. Others thought that being himself poor, as were most Italian noblemen at that time, he imagined that Ouida was a wealthy woman, and when he discovered his error cautiously withdrew from any promise he might have made. But despite Ouida's love of Italy and of its people she never fully understood the Latin temperament, which often indulges in amatory talk and letter-writing without any serious underlying meaning, nor did she perhaps realize that a man can be in love with a woman and yet not desire matrimony (especially when she is past her youth, and Ouida was thirty-one when she first met Stufa), or not sufficiently so to break entirely with old ties that have become an inveterate habit. And on the other hand, Ouida herself, notwithstanding the characters in and the subjects of her novels, that made them anathema to so many people in the seventies and early eighties of the nineteenth century, was in her own person eminently virtuous and respectable—a totally different thing from being unconventional—and would never have consented to enter into any irregular relationship. Yet it seems strange that, finding Stufa made no effort to demolish the obstacle that Ouida rightly or wrongly believed to exist, her pride and dignity did not cause her to accept the situation and bear her disappointment in silence. Temperaments differ, and an unfulfilled love may improve a woman's character, may widen her sympathies and deepen her capacity for feeling, may teach her what it means to care for another far more than for herself, or it may, and this undoubtedly is what more often happens, embitter and harden her, may narrow her sympathies, and intensify the self-absorption of a nature already too prone to make everything revolve round itself. And perhaps the secret of Ouida's infatuation is to be found in this very self-absorption. Her passion was possibly three parts begotten and fed by her own imagination, and in it, as in so many other things in her life, she lacked a sense of proportion. A woman may be very sure that when a man really cares deeply and sincerely for her and knows his love to be returned, he will find

OUIDA IN 1874.

Photograph by Adolphe Beau.

To face p. 89.

a way out of a previous entanglement, be it what it may. But Ouida never ceased to believe, and to find consolation in the belief, that Stufa was being kept away from her against his will, and that one day or other he would return to her and redeem the promise she considered him to have made.

The winter of 1874 seems to have been less gay than usual in Florence. In January Ouida wrote to Baron Tauchnitz :—

"Florence is very sad this season. Duels and misfortunes of all kinds. The gentlemen and the populace are at feud, and all go armed against each other like Guelfs and Ghibelins, so there will be no Carnival."

She was now writing *Signa*, a story of peasant-life in the part of Tuscany in which her villa was situated. The Marchese della Stufa, who knew the district well, helped her very greatly with the local colour. For the Tauchnitz edition she sent, at the Baron's request, a photograph of herself, to be engraved as a frontispiece. When the engraving was submitted to her, she wrote to Tauchnitz :—

"Florence,
"*December* 14 [1874].

"I like the portrait very much. There is only one fault, due, I think, to the American drawing—that the upper lip is much longer and straighter than my own is. I have been much pleased with it, however."

Signa was published in 1875.

Ouida : a Memoir

In the autumn Ouida had a bad attack of diphtheria, but was able to issue early in 1876 her novel, *In a Winter City*, dealing with society in Florence. She made the Duke of Albany's acquaintance and held a very high opinion of his abilities. When he died in 1884, she expressed in print her regret for the loss of one who would have done so much for the progress and appreciation of the arts in England. She was now writing her Roman novel, *Ariadne*, which, however, could not be published till the end of January, 1877, because she found it necessary to go to Rome in order to verify allusions and descriptions. It is in the letter to Tauchnitz in which she tells him this that we find the first hint of those financial difficulties that were now to pursue her to the end of her life. Although she was receiving large sums, as such payments went then, for her books, her manner of life required a princely income. In a letter dated August 22, 1876, in referring to some money difficulties due to other people's affairs, she wrote : " I have such a horror of pecuniary entanglements." She goes on to observe that " my fame has increased in England extraordinarily the last two years," and then proceeds to ask Baron Tauchnitz for an advance and to raise the honorarium for her forthcoming novel, *Ariadne*. From this time forward Ouida constantly asked him for advances, almost invariably requesting that the sum should be sent by return of post. Her petitions met with generous response. Tauchnitz's forbearance and kindness do honour to the profession to which he belongs.

Ouida now became extremely exigent with regard to the details of the publication of her books, and her letters show her many anxieties regarding the fit way in which they should be presented to the public, and incidentally her exalted opinion of her own work. She asked Tauchnitz not to advertise *Ariadne* until it was nearly ready.

Ouida to Baron Tauchnitz.

"*October* 2, 1876.

"I find that when the public knows the name of a work long beforehand it takes off its freshness, wears out speculations concerning it, and altogether spoils its success."

In February, 1877, she went to Rome in order to verify certain passages in *Ariadne*, where she had a delightful and brilliant time "at Court and Embassies, etc.," she wrote to Tauchnitz. Her growing fame on the Continent was attested by a portrait in a Leipzig paper.

Ouida to Baron Tauchnitz.

[*March*, 1877.]

"The woodcut is too dreadful. It is a fat, sensual-looking creature, and a kind of union between a cook and a Bacchante."

Comments on public affairs abound in the letters.

Ouida : a Memoir

Ouida to Baron Tauchnitz.

"*April* 24, 1877.

"I fear we are fairly lancé on war. Your oracle of Varzin might still prevent it, and England might have done with ease a few months ago. Palmerston used to say Gladstone ' would go mad or ruin England.' He bids fair to do both."

At last *Ariadne* was published.

Ouida to Baron Tauchnitz.

[*June*, 1877.]

"*Ariadne* has a great success everywhere, and commands the homage of great artists who, after all, are the only people that can *really* understand it."

And in a later letter (October 14, 1877) she declares "*Ariadne* creates deep emotion in many people."

The book was dedicated "à mon amie, la Duchesse de Castiglione," and its Roman setting is delightful. The story, a very slight one, is marred by exaggeration, and shows a lack of proportion in estimating human character. But the novel is full of striking passages that deal with surprising insight either with scenery or with art, and clearly show Ouida's appreciation of beauty and her considerable powers of criticism and her independent, even if prejudiced, point of view.

Until now Ouida's books had been published by Chapman and Hall, but at the end of the year they

were transferred to the firm of Chatto and Windus.
Ouida declared that it was without her knowledge or
consent, and that she had refused Chatto's higher offers
three years previously, in order to stay with her old
friends, Chapman and Hall. Mr. Chatto went out to
Florence to see her, and matters were amicably settled.
M. Buloz, the editor of the *Revue des Deux Mondes*,
paid her a visit this year. French translations of two of
her early stories had [1] appeared in the *Revue* in 1868 ;
in 1873, the " Branch of Lilac," one of the stories in
A Dog of Flanders, was similarly published. Ouida's
work was then much appreciated in France, partly
because of her sympathy with the nation in its misfortunes, and also because of its " qualités littéraires :
l'esprit souple, mordant, independant, aventureux,
une grâce à part, mondaine et cavalière." Thus
writes the French critic in a brief preface to the
translation. He also says that she scandalized her
countrymen and women, " par des audaces dont ils
n'ont pas l'habitude. Certes les Dickens et les
Thackeray auxquels on l'accuse de se croire supérieure,
eussent hésité devant les sujets qu'elle choisit volontiers ;
on va jusqu'à lui attribuer cette réponse caractéristique
faite à ceux qui la blâmaient d'alarmer ses chastes
lectrices par le dédain du mariage et par des peintures
trop vives des entraînemens du cœur ou trop indul-
gentes des faiblesses masculines : ' Je n'écris pas pour
les femmes, j'écris pour les militaires.' "

[1] See p. 34.

Ouida : a Memoir

At the end of 1877 her banker went off in debt a million and a half and at sixty-five years of age eloped with a ballet-girl. It caused her some awkwardness in pecuniary matters, but they were soon righted. The next year she published her novel *Friendship*, the *roman à clef* in which she told her own love-story from her own point of view. Her friends tried to dissuade her from publishing the book. She answered them that a writer of celebrity could not " be limited to the ideas and the limits of a few Florentine opinions."

Its appearance was the beginning of her troubles in Florence, and brought her the bitter resentment of those persons who considered themselves drawn to the life in the novel. They were influential people who had it in their power to make life in Florence very unpleasant for Ouida. Florence, indeed, was divided into two parties : pro-Ouidaites and anti-Ouidaites. She made no pretence of conciliation, and writing to Claud Harding, January 12, 1881, said, "Everything in *Friendship* IS TRUE as solemnly as I can declare it." In England the significance of the book was scarcely grasped and the critics reviewed it as an ordinary novel and one not up to Ouida's usual standard. Ouida herself thought that the early chapters of *Friendship* contained her best work. Few, if any, will agree with her to-day.

The doubtful reception of the book in Florence led Ouida to withdraw herself to a great extent from society, seeing only a few intimate friends. But the

OUIDA IN 1878.

From a crayon drawing by Alice Danyell.

To face p. 95.

flow of visitors from England who wished to make her acquaintance was unceasing, and she was always willing to receive persons of rank, distinction, and importance.

In the summer of 1878 Mrs. Danyell [1] drew a crayon portrait of Ouida, which appeared with a notice containing extravagant praise in the *Whitehall Review* for October 5, 1878. The original drawing was much altered by the engravers, and Ouida was justly indignant.

Ouida to Mrs. Danyell.

[1878.]

"You are far too lenient to the horrid portrait ; your picturesque graceful drawing is entirely effaced ! —yet I made it a condition that it should be followed line for line. Did ever you see such dogs ?—they would suit a vivisector's portrait."

The hot months of this year were spent in Austria, a country of which Ouida was very fond.

Tauchnitz kept her well supplied with the new English novels, and she criticized them freely in her letters to him. She found that English novelists paid too little attention to symmetry and strength of structure. Moreover, Ouida had a way of discovering that other novelists took their stories from hers. She considered that the *motif* of *The First Violin* was taken from

[1] Daughter of Cavaliere Tassinari.

Under Two Flags. She thought it was written by two hands, the German and musical part being very clever, "the girl's portion poor and rather vulgar."

Ouida's method of working illustrates her general extravagance. She used sheets of a large size foolscap paper, writing on it lengthwise in her large sprawling hand. These she threw unnumbered on to the floor or anywhere out of her way as she worked and never looked at them again until the proofs came. Her way with proofs is well illustrated in the following note to Mr. Frederic Harrison on receiving from him proofs of an address delivered by him during the Boer War and published by the South African Conciliation Committee.

"*November* 10 [1900].

"DEAR SIR,—

"Accept my thanks for your kind reply.

"Proofs are to me an immense joy; they are the wet clay to the sculptor, and my own thoughts sometimes wear to me a wholly different aspect when I see them in type.

"I beg to remain,

"Yours obliged,

OUIDA."

She sometimes demanded as many as seven consecutive revises of one book. Needless to say that her publishers' views on proofs did not coincide with hers.

First Years in Florence

It may be mentioned here that her extravagant spirit showed itself in another way. To the end of her life, even in days of direst poverty, she used most expensive writing-paper and envelopes, in earlier years decorated with a large monogram formed of the five letters of the name Ouida. The same monogram also appears on some of the title-pages of the first editions of her early novels.

Ouida's literary work from 1870 to 1878 comprised eight novels and a volume of short stories. Among these are *Pascarèl*, *Signa*, and *Ariadne*, which with *In Maremma*, to be published in 1882, form the quartette of Italian novels, the best work she ever did and on which, with some of her short stories, her literary reputation must rest. To this decade also belongs *The Dog of Flanders* and the other stories in that volume, and *Two Little Wooden Shoes*, a pathetic and prettily written tale, spoilt by an absurdly overdrawn lurid scene at the end. In *In a Winter City*, which is of course Florence, Ouida gives a picture of Florentine society in the seventies, but so much imagination is mingled with her description that the book is less interesting than might be expected. The period was ended by *Friendship*, the *roman à clef* which so greatly harmed Ouida's social career.

These years were undoubtedly the time of Ouida's greatest vogue. One proof of this may be found in Sir F. C. Burnand's parody of *Strathmore* as *Strapmore! a Romance, by Weeder*, which appeared in *Punch* in 1878. It extends to eighteen chapters, and burlesques in most diverting fashion both the novels of society and the Italian peasant stories.

IV

LATER YEARS
IN FLORENCE
1879—1894

CHAPTER IV

LATER YEARS IN FLORENCE
1879—1894

OUIDA'S friendship with Baron Tauchnitz had grown closer, and in December, 1878, he began a practice of sending her a Dresden china figure as a Christmas gift. This time it was a shepherd.

Ouida to Baron Tauchnitz.

"*January* 16, 1879.

"You have exactly divined my greatest weakness— rare china! and the lovely Saxe shepherd is one of the most exquisite figures that I ever saw. Once more accept my heartfelt thanks for the pleasure you have given me—a twofold pleasure in the object itself and in the kind friendship that sent it me."

[*June* 25, 1879.]

"Your beautiful little shepherd is smiling at me from a Louis XV writing-table, and is much admired."

Next Christmas Tauchnitz sent a shepherdess to match the shepherd.

Ouida : a Memoir

In May, 1880, Ouida had a bad attack of bronchitis, an illness to which she was subject throughout her life, and was for a time in danger. Her recovery was slow and difficult. Her novel *Moths* was published this year, and the hero was probably based on Mario. The story was dramatized by Henry Hamilton and produced at the Globe Theatre, London, March 25, 1883. It made a very effective play ; the leading part was taken by Mrs. Bernard Beere.

Ouida felt that a change was necessary before her health could be entirely restored, and contemplated a visit to Rome. She was weak and depressed and easily worried. The woman engaged to take care of the house and the dogs while she and her mother were away failed at the last moment. Indeed, her difficulties with her servants, except with Gori, the maid, who was faithful to her to the last, were always more or less acute. On one occasion, when she had contemplated a visit to Germany, she wrote to Mrs. Danyell :—

"To your surprise no less than to mine I am still here ! The week before last, as I was just about to join friends at Homburg, the servant you recognized, furious (I suppose) at having been given warning, rushed on me with a great broom-handle three inches round and attempted to brain me. I threw up my left arm and caught the blow *slanting* on that ; if it had come down straight it must have broken the bone ; as it was, it has given me a bad blow, so that to-day is the first time I can wear a sleeve. I couldn't travel with it. I hear that the man did stab a person in Florence and went to prison for it."

To the same correspondent she wrote on the occasion of the contemplated visit to Rome :—

Ouida to Mrs. Danyell.

"*January*, 1881.

"I am very sick at heart of such perpetual disappointment : of course, I could go alone, but my mother wants change much and it seems unkind to leave her alone. . . . The only thing that makes me doubt about Rome is that it will look like *following* him." [1]

She told her friends, the Tassinari :—
"The days seem so blank and strange here [2] without seeing his face ; life is death to me. . . . I always feel so much better when near him."

And so Ouida overcame her scruples, if ever she really had any, and spent two months in Rome. Before her departure from Florence she wrote to Baron Tauchnitz the letter containing the famous sentence about herself and George Eliot.

[1] *I.e.*, Stufa, who was on duty at the Quirinal as gentleman-in-waiting to King Humbert and Queen Margherita.
[2] In Florence.

Ouida : a Memoir

" January 10 [1881].

" I find *Endymion* very poor stuff, and were it by
an unknown author no one would buy it. What a
state the British Government is in !

" I hope to go to Rome in a week or so for the
month of Carnival. I cough still and want some
change of air and of society. . . .

" English literature is very sorry stuff nowadays.
You must make much of *me*, for now George Elliott [1]
is gone there is no one else who can write English."

The visit to Rome occupied February and March,
and Ouida, notwithstanding the break, for Stufa no
longer took any notice of her, found a delight in
being near him.

Mme. Ramé did not accompany her daughter,
but remained behind to look after the villa and all
the numerous pets and plants that demanded careful
attention. It was the first time that the mother
and daughter had been separated, and Mme. Ramé
wrote almost daily letters, giving Ouida all the home
news and expressing her adoring affection. Great
efforts were made that Ouida might cut a distinguished
figure in Roman society. Much time and thought
were expended on her clothes, and one of the Italian
servants went with her to act as lady's-maid. Mme.
Ramé, however, with all her adoration of her daughter,
took a wise view of the Stufa affair, and gently told

[1] So spelt by Ouida.

her that it would be more dignified on her part not to run after him, since his manner of acting went to prove that he was not sufficiently in love to overcome whatever were the obstacles in his path. Ouida's reckless expenditure was evidently beginning to tell, for there are many references in Mme. Ramé's letters to the scarcity of money. "With the greatest care," she writes on one occasion, "money will make itself wings in housekeeping."

Ouida wrote constantly to the Tassinari family of her doings in Rome, and over and over again refers to Stufa :—

"He has a wonderfully good position in Rome, and people adore him. He has his suite of rooms in the Palace, and every one is in raptures over his courtesies and grace. . . . He looked so well at the Royal ball on Monday ; they placed me in the seats for foreigners of distinction in front of the throne ; then, when the Queen moved and people were free to move too, I sat in the Circle of the Ambassadresses. I could not but think of his being told no decent woman would know me ! ! It is very beautiful weather here ; last night as I drove home from the French Embassy, Rome looked Ariadne's Rome— made of silver and ivory. . . .

"My rooms look on the Storys' garden, and I am constantly with them. I see a good deal of the Pagets and the Noailles."

Ouida : a Memoir

Ouida to Claud Harding.

" ROME,

" *February* 23, 1881.

" Pray never give the curiosity of those *people* any *biographical materials* ; the less said to them or their kind the better. Rome is brilliant as usual. My mother stays with her flowers and dogs, while I pass some months here. . . . [Stufa] is in waiting all this time, but he is so fearfully changed that he has nothing of what he once was, save his perfect manner. . . . I go to Court and all the great balls, for the sake of 'what the world says,' but society is sadder than solitude with him for ever before me. . . . The ball last night at the German Embassy was the grandest, I think, of this year. . . . The Royal balls are ill-managed and dull, and we all catch cold, the Quirinal is so draughty."

Ouida to Mrs. Danyell.

" ROME [*March*, 1881].

" I see the Queen en tête-à-tête to-morrow ; of course, I have seen her at all the great parties, but not to have a long conversation. . . . The Paget ball was brilliant ; very exclusive, as even the Royal list was much cut down."

When the Roman visit had long been a thing of the past, Ouida wrote to Mrs. Danyell :—

" I hear the Queen spoke of me the other day with

increased kindness and interest ; this must *tell*, and her friendship is most valuable. How far off it seems, all that brilliant life of Rome ! "

She returned to Florence at the end of March and in June fell ill with peritonitis and spent two months in bed. In August she was still very ill, and in September told Tauchnitz that the expenses of the illness were very burdensome and asked for an advance :

" I had to pay to-day my 3,000 francs [1] of rent, which in this country one must always pay for the year to come, which is very unjust, as one might never live to inhabit the house. I wish you would come to Florence and see me. This villa would delight you, and now the weather is cool it is a paradise."

For some time Ouida had been engaged on an Italian novel of a new character. It was entitled *A Village Commune*, and was the first of a number of novels and tales in which she fulminated against the oppression of the peasants by the Italian Government and against what she considered the vandalisms that were being carried out in the land. She expressed her views, not only in her novels, but also in articles in magazines and in letters to newspapers. Thus she brought on herself the hatred of the officials of the country, and even of persons in high places. She was well aware of it, for she wrote to a friend :—

" I suspect the sovereigns here are irritated at my

[1] £120.

Times letters, but I would rather write in *The Times* than please all the crowned heads of Europe."

Her well-wishers in Florence tried in vain to restrain her, but to their pleading she only answered :—

" I have always occupied myself with politics at intervals—once in London I wrote what threw a Bill out of the Commons, and you know how rare it is for a writer to turn the votes in England. But I think they don't here in the least understand my power."

She was obsessed with an idea of her extraordinary influence in European politics, and she used to talk seriously of the men she should select for ambassadors at different Courts. She fully believed that her place in history would be with Semiramis, Aspasia, Cleopatra, Mme. de Staël, and others of similar fame.

She was, however, wholly sincere in espousing the cause of the Italian peasants, and she really hoped to help the Italian lower classes by her writings.

Ouida to Claud Harding.[1]

" Ireland is in a frightful state ; it wants military law ; it is nothing less than criminal in a Government to allow any nation to think murder is legal and patriotic. I would have shot every second man on Mountmorris estates unless they had given up the murderer. But Parliament is only a clumsy govern-

[1] About 1881.

ing machine after all, and unhappily seldom represents the national will.

. . . . .

" I am now printing a story of the Italian people, who suffer far more than the Irish and say nothing."

The story was *A Village Commune*. In the appendix she wrote :—

"No one can accuse me of any political prejudices. My writings have alternately been accused of a reactionary conservatism and a dangerous socialism, so that I may, without presumption, claim to be impartial : I love conservatism when it means the preservation of beautiful things ; I love revolution when it means the destruction of vile ones.

" What I despise in the pseudo-liberalism of the age is that it has become only the tyranny of narrow minds, veiled under high-sounding phrases, and the deification of a policeman. I would give alike to a Capucin as to a Communist, to a Mormon as to a monk, the free choice of his opinions and mode of life. But this true liberty is nowhere to be found in Europe, and still less to be found in America ; and this pseudo-liberty meddles with every phase of private life and would dictate the rule of every simple act.

. . . . .

" I know the Italian people well ; I mean the poor, the labouring people. I am attached to them for their lovableness, their infinite natural intelligence, their wondrous patience ; they are a material of which much might be made.

" They are but little understood by foreigners, even by foreign residents ; they are subtle and yet simple, of an infinite good-nature, and yet sadly selfish ; they are very docile, yet they have great sensitiveness, and I see no more greed in them than in the poor of all countries. . . . There are sundry people, very, very poor, to each of whom I give a little sum weekly ; *not one* of these people has ever asked for more than the allotted sum, not one has ever made it an excuse to plead for further gifts.

" ' How can you write books about these *birbonaccie* ? ' said an Italian nobleman to me, meaning about the contadini in *Signa*. ' They spend their whole lives in fleecing us. You should never believe a word that they say.' "

Ruskin took the same view as Ouida, and in his *Art of England* [1] wrote :—

" There is probably no more oppressed, no more afflicted order of gracious and blessed creatures—God's own poor, who have not yet received their consolation—than the mountain peasantry of Tuscany and Romagna. What their minds are, and what their state, and what their treatment, those who do not know Italy may best learn, if they can bear the grief of learning it, from Ouida's photographic story of *A Village Commune*."

[1] 1883.

Later Years in Florence

A Village Commune roused great animosity against her. One person who thought himself the butt of her pen threatened to tear her out of her carriage the next time he saw her, and on one occasion she was certainly shot at when driving back to Scandicci from Florence, and only the skill of her coachman prevented the ponies from bolting.

"I don't think the men meant to shoot *me*," she wrote to the Tassinari, "but they were close to the pony's head and fired; probably in brutal scherzo. It was quite daylight. They were roughs. I shall not imitate other people by making a fuss about it."

But this antagonism to the laws of the land in which she lived, and to those whose duty it was to execute them, had far-reaching consequences, for, on the least provocation, Ouida would appeal to justice. If a muzzling order for dogs was issued, if her dogs frightened people or bit children, if her servants misbehaved themselves, if a tradesman in her opinion overcharged her, she went to law. She invariably lost the case, and not only had to pay the sum in dispute but heavy lawyers' bills in addition. Sometimes even she would call in another lawyer to fight the one she had previously employed. It was such lawsuits on the top of her reckless personal extravagance that crippled her resources and ultimately brought her to ruin.

Notwithstanding these distractions, the practice of

her art filled the greater part of her time. When Claud Harding sent her a manuscript asking her opinion on it, her reply forms sensible criticism on the art of writing in general, and serves also to illustrate her own opinion of herself.

Ouida to Claud Harding.

"*December* 16, 1881.

"Composition is a great Art, like painting or music, and requires a life absolutely dedicated to it, also continual study of classic and other literature. I know, as you justly observe, that nine-tenths of the tales in periodicals are very silly and weak. But this is unfortunately because publishers do not know good writing ; and also that great writers require costlier payments than magazines can afford to give. Un-luckily, almost every one thinks he or she can write, whereas Literature is, believe me, an art and a difficult one, like music or sculpture. Even the common fluency of common prose writers is only to be acquired by study and continual practice. I was 'born to write' as larks to sing ; but I have destroyed probably three times as much MS. as I have printed. Balzac did the same ; only he more wasteful, tore up proofs. I shall always be most happy to answer you, and only hope you will not feel to me as the Archbishop did to Gil Blas. I say what I think—but then I am not infallible."

Later Years in Florence

Similarly characteristic is the following extract from a letter to *The Times*, entitled " English Novels," in May, 1882 :—

" My own name is fully as well known from Tobolsk to Tangier as that of Cherbuliez or Alphonse Daudet.

. . . . .

" The greatest injury to the novel is, in my opinion, the *feuilleton* form (in France) and the serial form (in England), which so often precedes publication as a whole: in it the writer sacrifices form and harmony to the object of attaining an exciting fragment for each division of his work."

With middle age Ouida's sense of her dignity and importance, which had been placed by her very high from the first, increased.

Ouida to Baron Tauchnitz.

[*March*, 1882.]

" Please to address me Madame de la Ramé or Madame Ouida at all times."

When the Baron asked the reason of this desire she replied :—

" I cannot tell you all my reasons—but even if I had none, it is the more correct way to address a woman of eminence. You always see MME. Sarah Bernhardt."

She was at this time about to publish a volume of children's stories entitled *Bimbi*, and in asking

Tauchnitz to take them declared : "Whatever I wrote would be read with the same eagerness."

The Royal Family of Italy had shown Ouida much kindness, and she dedicated *Bimbi* to "S.A.R. Vittorio Emanuele Principe di Napoli." The stories are excellent.[1] The first, "The Nürnberg Stove," is full of charm and pathos ; another, "Meleagris Gallopavo," is a capital animal story, which foreshadows Rostand's *Chantecler*. Another, "The Little Earl," had been written for a small boy of Ouida's acquaintance, and she sent him the book with this note :—

" DEAR BERTIE,—Here is the book. Like a loyal subject, vous rendez place au Prince in your rights to the Little Earl. Perhaps some day when he is King and you are his grand scudiere you and he will talk of me and tell your children of Ouida."

The boy in question was Herbert Danyell, Cavaliere Tassinari's little grandson, to whom Ouida took a great fancy. At her request the boy was often sent to visit her, and the days spent at the Villa Farinola with her and her dogs and horses were some of the happiest of his childhood. It was in the "Rondo" at the back of the villa that he was first put on a horse, an event a child never forgets. But what made those days so delightful were the

[1] The book was translated into French for the " Bibliothèque Rose."

1883

Toga Virilis

Bonbons

Boisson
Sirupeuse
Gracieuse
Dorée

The Choice of Hercules

A PEN DRAWING BY OUIDA.

stories that Ouida used to tell him as they sat in one of the shady nooks of the gardens or under some tree by the river. Thus the little boy heard such tales as "The Little Earl," [1] and "Birds in the Snow," [2] and many others long before any one else read them in print. Ouida's harsh voice always became soft and pleasing when she spoke to children. She taught this boy to love and appreciate the sights and sounds of nature, and awoke his imagination. "To Ouida," he says, "I owe the joy of knowing that there is no such thing as loneliness as long as there are woods and moors and rivers and mountain brooks."

The drawing, "The Choice of Hercules," was made by Ouida for Bertie Danyell when it was decided that he was old enough to discard sailor suits and assume trousers and the ordinary clothes of growing youth. She was distressed to find that the child was developing so fast, and the boy feared he might now be considered too old to eat the bonbons with which Ouida liberally provided him.

There is no evidence that Ouida had a general love for children, but she took fancies to them now and again, as she did to grown-up people, and was always anxious to inculcate in them a love for animals [3] and for nature.

[1] In *A Dog of Flanders and Other Stories.*
[2] In *Pipistrello and Other Stories.*
[3] See pp. 307–309.

Ouida : a Memoir

To the same year belongs *In Maremma*, one of Ouida's best novels. The plot is more concentrated ; the action, though slight, is swifter, and there is a unity and a harmony of composition scarcely to be met elsewhere in her books. Indeed, were it not that, as usual, it is spoiled by an absurd Ouida-esque scene at the end, it would take high rank as a piece of literature. Leaving the story aside, the book breathes the very spirit of the locality : we feel as if we had actually lived there among its people. The heroine, Musa, is delightful in her freshness, simplicity, and dignity. For once Ouida seems to have been wholly the artist, and to have created a heroine who is not merely the embodiment of her idealization of herself.

The book abounds in charming passages. As an example we may take the following :—

" ' Do you ever think that I shall die ? ' she[1] said abruptly to the child, who looked at her in some surprise.

" ' Die ? ' she echoed. ' That is going away into the earth, you mean, as everything does, and then it goes upward and lives with God, they say ; would you wish that ? '

" ' I will have to do it whether I wish or not, and about living with God I do not know. I am a sinful soul, though not worse than most. But you do not

---

[1] Chap. iv. Joconda had adopted and brought up Musa, the daughter of a brigand of the district.

understand. When I am dead, under the earth, as you say, what will you do ? '

" ' I do not know.'

" She did not, she had never thought of the matter ; her mind was blank, though her body was vigorous. Then she added, after a little thought :—

" ' I will give myself to the sea ; that is the way I will die.'

" ' You ! I speak of myself.'

" ' I will die if you do.'

" Joconda looked at her amazed and keenly touched.

" ' Do you love me so much then ? ' she cried suddenly.

" ' Is that love ? ' said the child. ' I should not like to live if you were not here ; I do not know if you call that love.'

" ' It is love,' said Joconda.

" She felt her eyes full of the slow tears of age —tears salt as the crystals the sea left on the shore. ' Ah, my dear, my dear ! ' she muttered, ' it is not myself that will cause you to die for love, but it may be some other—when I am gone and cannot help you ! Ah, child ! why were you born ?'

" Musa did not hear ; she was standing with her brown hand on the white head of her dog, looking out seaward ; the words that had been spoken had not saddened her because they were vague to her. Joconda had always been there—why should she go away to earth or sky ? "

Ouida's ardent love of nature and her close observation of its processes are well brought out in this book. There is a wonderful description [1] as seen from the Maremma of " that miracle—perhaps of all the greatest miracle—of nature, the migration of the winged nations of the air." We might almost be reading White's *Selborne*.

Meanwhile her life continued its usual way, and she wrote often to Tauchnitz.

Ouida to Baron Tauchnitz.

[*May* 27, 1882.]

" I wish you could see this house ; it is such a grand old place and so much wood around it, so rare a blessing in Italy."

[*August* 6, 1882.]

" I am much interested in Egypt ; England is quite right, and I only hope she will go through with the matter and make a Protectorate there."

On some great occasion Ouida would issue from her semi-seclusion.

Ouida to Baron Tauchnitz.

[*November*, 1882.]

" We have had our Royal people here, and they gave one very pretty soirée, when old Pitti looked

[1] Chap. xiv.

very grand lighted up—but, alas! things are bad with the country in general and the foreign policy execrable."

To her friends the Tassinari she wrote on the same occasion :—

"It was very pretty last night and the Palazzo Pitti looked beautiful. After the reception we had a concert. There were only the Italian nobility present; no foreigners save myself, the Duc de Dino, and Talleyrand. The King and Queen were very kind; the King told me three times to be sure and go to Rome in this winter. How beautiful the Sala degli Stucchi is lighted up! it is the noblest room in Europe. The Queen looked very pretty in a cream and carnation brocade with her thirteen rows of pearls."

Her letters now show that her mind was much occupied with public affairs.

Ouida to Captain Danyell.

[1882.]

"I fear they are muffing Egypt after all. Arabi should have been shot in the twenty-four hours; now the war will come over again in a few years' time."

"This superb swift course of victory recalls the campaigns of Alexander rather than any prosaic modern warfare. I condone Gladstone's previous sins in view of his having had the sense and courage to trust Garnet Wolseley. . . .

Ouida : a Memoir

" The gain of England in this war is the world's gain, for it means a death-blow to Moslem revolt and bigotry and a deep wound to all radicalism, socialism, and nihilism throughout the earth."

She gave expression to her feelings in the following lines, which were published in *The Times*, September 5, 1882 [1] :—

> "Great England put her armour by, and stretch'd
> Her stately limbs to slumber in the sun.
> The nations, seeing then how long she slept,
> Commun'd together, and in whispers said :
> 'Lo! She is old and tired ; let us steal
> The crown from off her brows. She will not know !'
> And Goneril and Regan, over seas,
> Mocking her, cried : 'Her time is past. Her blood
> Is sluggish, and her rusted sword from out
> Her scabbard she will draw no more !' And so,
> Thus gibing, flung with cruel hands the seeds
> Of discord and of hate amidst her sons.
> But from the East there came a blast too loud,
> As from the West there came a taunt too much ;
> And she, awaking, rais'd her head, and saw
> Around her all her faithless friends, and all
> Her sisters and her children jeering her,
> And crying 'She is old !' and meting out
> Her lands amongst themselves, and parcelling
> Her honour. Then, swift as lightning flashes
> From blue skies, her glance of scorn fell on them,
> And they crouch'd, like wolves that are o'ermastered.
> England stretch'd out her hand, and touch'd the world—
> England arose, and spake, and calmly said :
> 'Nay ! I am mistress still.'"

[1] Reprinted here by kind permission.

Later Years in Florence

Ouida to Baron Tauchnitz.

January 3 [1883].

" What a strange thing, Gambetta's death !—it is very like arsenical poisoning—so was mine,[1] but we could prove nothing. He was a great enemy to Germany—but for France I imagine it will be a calamity, because I fear the Republicans will fly to some more violent communist as a leader, and then the mad destroying fires may spread beyond French frontiers."

[*January* 23, 1883.]

" How France is disgracing herself ! Bismarck is quite right in thinking that while she is Republican she will be always miserably disunited and weak."

[*March* 1, 1883.]

" All these troubles in England and France make the fortunes of us poor *rentiers* very overshadowed. I am, I confess, very disturbed at the state of England. There is a curious apathy in the whole of the country which renders it unfit to meet the severe trials of the present crisis."

Wanda, dedicated to Lady Paget, some of whose traits are to be found in the heroine of *In a Winter City*, was published in 1883. The scene is laid in the Austrian Tyrol, a district which Ouida greatly loved. Information about the Austrian pride of race, on which

[1] Ouida refers here to her own illness, see p. 107.

the story mainly turns, was given Ouida by her friend Mrs. Callander, and Tauchnitz helped her with the German words and expressions.

The same year she contributed a letter on "Romance and Realism" to *The Times* (October 12) which is reprinted in *Frescoes*, a collection of dramatic sketches also issued in 1883.

She was enlarging her circle of friends and renewing older acquaintances. There are numerous references in her letters to Lord Lytton,[1] to whom, after Stufa's defection, she seems to have transferred her adoration. She had probably first known him in London in 1867 and 1870. He spent April and May, 1884, in Florence. She wrote to Baron Tauchnitz in June, 1884 :—

"Would you kindly send me Robert, Lord Lytton's *Poems and Fables*? He has been much with me of late, and I am anxious to study his printed thoughts."

Newer acquaintances were Sir Rennell Rodd and Earl Curzon of Kedleston. She was introduced to the former when a young man of one or two and twenty at Florence, and then he met her in London in 1887. After that time they never met again, but about 1893 Ouida began to write to him spasmodically. When he was in Rome (1901–1904) she wrote often, confiding her affairs, which were then in very bad case, to him, and he was of much assistance to her. After he left Rome she wrote to him constantly, and learning

[1] Owen Meredith.

her difficulties from other sources, he got a group of friends quite quietly to help a little through Mr. Carmichael, the British Consul at Leghorn. Ouida wrote an article on Rennell Rodd's poems, which she greatly admired.

Lord Curzon first made her personal acquaintance when he went to lunch with her at the Villa Farinola on Easter Sunday, 1885. From that time Ouida wrote fairly regularly to him, and about all things that interested her. She wrote of dogs and animals, breathing her fierce resentment against the muzzling of dogs in England when rabies had to be stamped out ; she expressed her unreasoning hostility to certain British statesmen of whom she would admit no good. She greatly sympathized with Lord Curzon's efforts in India to preserve and restore the monuments of earlier ages, and in reply to some remarks in which he had denounced the native fashion of smearing over the most exquisite fabrics and sculpture with white-wash, and the atrocities committed in that country by military engineers, wrote in 1900 [1] :—

" Were the names altered from Hindostanee to Italian, what you say might read as a record of the barbarisms of our Communes. It is a piteous sight all the world over and greed is the chief motor-power. Would that whitewash had never been known ! No sooner is a noble and ancient building taken for any public office than the army of daubers is set to work.

[1] From Lucca.

123

Military men are horrible destroyers everywhere ; but here engineers and contractors are the worst of all. There is nothing in existing education or influences to inspire good taste or reverence for the past."

When Lord Curzon in 1905 resigned the Viceroyalty of India, Ouida wrote to him in great sympathy and indignation ; and among her papers when she died were found, carefully preserved, a draft telegram to him in her handwriting[1] and Lord Curzon's reply.[2]

"VICEREGAL LODGE, SIMLA,
"*September* 27, 1905.

"MY DEAR OUIDA,—

"How very good of you to have thought of me from your Italian retreat. My resignation, after much that I had experienced, was one of the happiest and proudest moments of my public life : and I leave India a happy man, my work for the most part done—and most of the harvest in the barn. How seldom we can feel this !

"I deserve congratulation therefore rather than solace !

"Yours sincerely,
"CURZON."

[1] It runs : "Congratulate you and the country on your decision. —OUIDA."

[2] The letter is endorsed "Private," and is printed here by Earl Curzon's kind permission.

Later Years in Florence

Such a letter bears eloquent testimony to the estimation in which Ouida's intelligence was held by those who were in touch with her and could sympathize with her aims and ideals. In the declining years of her life, when Ouida was destitute and lonely, Lord Curzon was prominent among those who rendered her generous assistance.

Between 1885 and 1887 Ouida used sometimes to go and see Eugene Lee-Hamilton, who was at that time an invalid and living with his half-sister, Vernon Lee. They were much exercised by Ouida's absurd appearance in her white satin garb, and found her talk dull or even worse, for she liberally emphasized her preference for "gens du monde" over authors and artists.

Only a few impressions of those who visited her at Farinola at this period are available. Mr. A. L. Woodroffe went out to lunch with her one cold day in March, taking with him Wills, the dramatist. His impression was of a woman with a tallowy complexion, straight black hair, red nose, dressed in a décolleté gown of blue glistening silk, covered with lace resembling a curtain, the skirt very short to display her beautiful feet, cased in blue satin shoes. She was surrounded by dogs, who never left her for a moment. Wills was a raconteur, but with a slow manner. He was telling a tale when Ouida turned aside to feed one of the dogs. Wills stopped. When Ouida had finished, she asked Wills, " Why don't you go on ? " "Oh!" he replied, "I won't interrupt the dog." When her visitors left, Ouida accompanied them part of the way back, walking through the meadows in her strange costume, and gathering for them the big red anemones which grew there in profusion.

Miss Maria Grant, the novelist, who saw Ouida in Florence,[1] thus records her impressions of the woman and her surroundings. They are worth quoting at length because they testify to Ouida's powers of conversation, so often depreciated.

"That sweet, fair, restful place, with its encircling woods and 'choir of birds,' and its lovely, sunlit landscape. In the distance, blue dreamy hills and green shadowy valleys and soft fertile plains; and in the foreground the gray tower and ramparts of Certosa. . . . Who could ever forget hours spent at Farinola, or the vivid personality stamped on the whole place ? The sense of seclusion resting within its encircling walls, in the shelter of which dwell so many—old and young, strong and feeble, man and beast ! How vividly one recalls them all :—the picturesque dark-eyed Tuscan attendants, the great snow-white Maremma hounds, lying in the winter sunshine on the marble steps or in the warmth of the fire-glow in the crimson, satin-lined, miniature room. The sense of beauty everywhere, so satisfying and so complete. The cool, softly-shaded hall, full of

[1] Cf. *Cara Roma*, by Miss Grant, vol. ii., 1885.

towering palms and green fernery, where we sat
often in converse during the hot bright hours of
the day, watching the sun gleam on the blue hills
in the distance, and listening to the birds' glad choral
in the woods below. And the large darker room, the
beautiful shadowy dining-room, where we circled round
the cosy home-like table for tea, and where, as the chill
of the short winter day crept on, the great logs burnt
cheerily in the wide chimney-corner. And then the
ever kindly welcome from the sweet, old, bright-eyed
lady who presides over that home, and from *her*, the
centre of all, who dwells so quietly there, and whom
people of all climes and nations come from all regions
of the earth to see. And then the bright memory of
those hours of converse! The vivid imagination
illuminating the dullness of one's own, like a fire-
flash in a dusky corner ; the sparkling, satirical, and
yet playful and sunny wit ; the intellect, so quick, so
clear, so 'fine' ; the wealth of literary and æsthetic
culture, the vast and versatile knowledge of the world
of many lands ; and, above all, that warm, kind
nature, so sympathetic, so intensely '*sensible*' to all
things that are beautiful and great and good, and at
the same time so acutely '*sensible*' to the pain and
the *lutte* and the passion of every created thing—of
every being that lives and that suffers—because, in all
nature, *pain* is the one inheritance that is inseparable
from life."

Mr. Lionel Robinson, a friend of long standing

and to whom she often submitted her novels in manuscript or proof, paid Ouida a visit at the villa. She asked him so to arrange his plans as to arrive at night, and told him to look out at the station for ponies with silver trappings. He complied with her wish, although, like most people, he preferred to arrive at a new and unknown place by daylight. Next day he asked Ouida her reason, and she replied that she wished his first impression of Farinola to be the view from it in the early morning.

In 1884 Ouida published *Pipistrello*, a collection of short stories, and *Princess Napraxine*, again a novel of society. *Othmar*, a sequel to it, was printed first as a feuilleton, a mode of publication Ouida detested.

Ouida to Baron Tauchnitz.

[*May* 1, 1885.]

" I hate feuilletons, but the times are so bad now, thanks to that madman Gladstone, that one is forced to accept many things one dislikes."

A letter to the Marchesa Incontri, formerly Princess Galitzin, shows what Ouida was thinking and doing at this time.

" *May* 17, 1885.

"I fear Canut [1] will suffer with the heat in that lowlying fortress ; if you write to his guardian, caution him never to walk him out when the sun is warm.

[1] A dog.

Later Years in Florence

Half the big dogs in Italy are killed by being dragged about in the heat. Ghino is merry and well ; his late mistress is gone and has sold her ponies and horses. . . .

"Are you writing any more Russian studies? There is no country more interesting, or qui a plus d'avenir. A very great English statesman, were there such a thing, would have seen the grandeur of an alliance which, giving Russia Constantinople and taking Afghanistan for Great Britain, would have laid the foundations of a durable accord and held the ambition of Germany in check. Politics have a great fascination for me. . . . All our friends are picnicking on wet grass in Royal company every day—it has rained incessantly all May. Everything looks luxuriant, but we get no strawberries."

When in 1885 Ouida urged Tauchnitz to issue more of her books, he told her—

"The sale of English literature on the Continent is so limited now, that we are inclined to reduce considerably the number of new publications, but your books are always welcome."

At this time Ouida began the custom of writing "topical" poems. She used to send them to her friends in England, asking that they would get them published in the British Press. On December 7, 1885, she sent Tauchnitz a poem entitled *The New Franchise*, and on the 10th wrote :—

"The poem was *not* for publication. When I have

more like it I will make a volume of them.[1] It did a great deal of good in England, but that dear country is in a bad way, being led by false prophets who only care for their own interests."

Among Ouida's visitors at the Villa Farinola was a boy who had been enchanted by her early novels as by beautiful and wonderful fairy-tales, a light in which they appeared to the young people of the late Victorian era. He was the Visconde George de Sarmento. When he came to Italy he felt he must meet Ouida, "the magician," and his mother therefore wrote to Ouida, who replied that she would be glad to see them. Ouida received them in her usual attitude, standing on a white bearskin rug dressed in pink satin with long white gloves. The boy expressed his admiration for her books. The visit was repeated the following year. But it was not until 1893, after she had left the Villa Farinola, that Ouida's close friendship with Sarmento began. She corresponded with him regularly until January 2, 1908. She wrote on an average four letters a month, and they touched on every conceivable subject. It is to Sarmento that we owe portraits of Ouida in her later years. He made three drawings of her, in 1895, 1896, and 1904. The first, in black and white chalk, he presented in 1909 to the Moyses Hall Museum, Bury St. Edmunds. The second, in red chalk, is in his own possession, and is here repro-

[1] This plan she never carried out.

duced by his special permission ; the third, also in red chalk, he presented to the National Portrait Gallery in 1908.[1]

Ouida spent the summer of 1886 at Homburg, and declared in the July of that year that she was so much occupied with English politics that she could attend to nothing else. Early in December Ouida went to London, where she stayed for five months, taking up her quarters again at the Langham Hotel, and enjoyed all the " 'grand mouvement' of such an interesting moment." Her mother did not accompany her, and Ouida wrote to her that she found herself "the idol of the great world." She met the Abercorns, Borthwicks, Sir John Millais, whom she frequently visited in his studio, and who made her laugh heartily on one occasion by quoting passages from Burnand's *Strapmore*, and other distinguished persons, and on April 1, 1887, dined at the House of Commons with the Home Secretary,[2] the President of the Board of Trade,[3] the Lord Advocate, and others. She was entertained at many of the great London houses : she was invited to Stafford House, *en petit comité*, when only a few persons of high rank and position were asked to meet her ; a party was

---

[1] Sarmento has kindly furnished much valuable information for this memoir. Under the pseudonym "George Vane" he is the author of two English novels. The scene of one of them, *A Love Dream* (1913), is Hardwick House, Bury St. Edmunds.

[2] H. Matthews.

[3] Sir Michael Hicks-Beach.

given in her honour at the French Embassy. The following extracts from letters to her mother during the visit to London show that she had a saner judgment of her own position than might be imagined from her usual utterances :—

" You will be amused that Hartington, having excited his imagination by *Ariadne*, was so disgusted with Rome that he exclaimed ' Why, it's no better than Dublin ! ' "

" Thank you so much for your unselfish pleasure in my social success. Unfortunately it costs so much ! ! —if I had only money. . . . Though London is so good to me, my opinion of the decay of England is, alas ! greatly confirmed. The Cabinet is a troop of unruly horses with no master mind amongst them. There is not *one* man who is a statesman or anything like it. Life here is not elegant nor is it enjoyed ; everybody is bored and in a hurry. The men are clever, but the cleverest are the most despairing and inert. The American women have the front rank, and though they are good-looking and agreeable they are very shallow and common at bottom. I do not in the least [deceive] myself as to the social adoration I receive, and I don't think they care two straws about intellect :—it is just now the fashion to come to me, and so my room fills with great people."

Later Years in Florence

Ouida to Mrs. Danyell.

[LONDON, 1887.]

" You will see by the papers that the weather is very bad here, but the houses are so warm and the society so delightful that it is far more agreeable than Florence, malgré the alternations of snow and fog. I am *always* warm here, and in Florence (in winter) never. The moment, too, is very interesting, and politically pregnant of great changes. Lord Orford's sister, Lady Dorothy Nevill, is at Sandringham, but I breakfast with her next week.

" My headquarters are in my old salon at the Langham Hotel, and my friends fill it with hothouse flowers."

Her " salon " at the Langham, well warmed and filled with rare hot-house flowers, the gifts of admiring friends, had quite an Italian atmosphere and formed a pleasing contrast to the inclement weather outside. A brilliant company was always to be found there, including, among others, Browning, Lord and Lady Lytton, Violet Fane, Oscar Wilde, Lady Dorothy Nevill, Winifred, Lady Howard of Glossop, Lady Llandaff, and Mr. Walter of *The Times*.

The visit to London, however, ended in gloom, and indeed resembled the passage of a brilliant meteor. For Ouida's financial resources did not warrant her extravagant expenditure, and she found herself practically stranded in London through her many

133

debts ; even her hotel bill was unpaid. It was then that Lady Dorothy Nevill, who characterized Ouida as one of the most hopelessly extravagant women she had ever known, aided by a few friends, came to her assistance and enabled her to return to Florence. She never again visited England. It may be stated here that the novelist's eccentricities and vagaries never impaired the pleasant relations that prevailed between her and Lady Dorothy Nevill, who kept up a correspondence with Ouida until the end, and was a staunch admirer of her best novels and tales.

On her return to Florence Ouida was still oppressed with financial difficulties. Notwithstanding that she had received £900 from Chatto and Windus in advance for *Guilderoy*, [1] in July she asked Tauchnitz for advances so that she might pay her rent due on June 1.

Ouida to Baron Tauchnitz.

" I am very much straightened in money matters just now, owing to my long absence. . . .

" My landlord will turn me out without any regard to the immense benefits I have done to his property ; indeed, he will be glad to get an excuse to let the place at an increased rental."

Tauchnitz, as usual, gave her some assistance.

---

[1] She declared the sum to be £400 less than usual, and that another firm had offered her £1,800. The book was published in 1889. See p. 150.

Later Years in Florence

In April, 1888, she was much grieved at Matthew Arnold's death ; his love of dogs and of nature and of calm drew her to him, and she composed some verses in his memory, sending a copy of them to Millais.

Ouida to Sir John Millais.

[FLORENCE, *April* 25, 1888.]

" I think you may like to have these lines on your dead friend, and I have sent them to *The Times*, but they may not perhaps have room for them.[1] I often think of your delicious studio and our pleasant hours. Lady Windsor has been here some months, and when she returns to London you must go and see her and talk of me."

The verses show feeling, and run thus :—

MATTHEW ARNOLD.

April, 1888.

O Kaï ! Thy master follows thee
Into the dread eternal night ;
He whose fair hope and aim was light
Has sunk beneath the moonless sea.

The scholar, poet, prophet, seer,
Is dead, as dead as Geist and Kaï.[2]
He whose heart thrilled at every cry
Lies deaf and blind upon his bier.

---

[1] *The Times* did not issue them. They are printed here for the first time by the kind permission of Miss Millais.

[2] Matthew Arnold's two dachshunds, to whom he was much attached.

Ouida : a Memoir

To him the torrent and the wold
As old familiar friends were dear.
The ocean far, the hill-side near,
Wak'd worship from his soul deem'd cold

By men who saw such little way
Into that clear and lofty mind
Which, mate to Plato's, still could find
Sport in a doggie's simple play.

The world is dark with war and greed,
Rebellion, anarchy, and lies ;
Ill can it spare his lessons wise,
Ill can it lose his classic creed.

Sweet lyrist in a noisy day,
Pure teacher of a vulgar crowd
Whose voice reach'd flutelike through the loud
Uproar of furious faction-frays.

The earth doth shake beneath the tread
Of armèd nations hot with lust
Of conquest, and no sword may rust
Within the scabbard lest the dread

Of rising peoples scare the sleep
From rich men's couch, from monarch's bed ;
And he who in sweet numbers wed
Wisdom with grace, he whom we weep

To-day, who call'd the weary age
To rest by the Pierian fount
Deep in wild-thyme on Hybla's mount
To hear the singer and the sage—

He whom we mourn to-day is dead,
As dead as humble Geist and Kaï.
Gone from the living world for aye,
The one Greek soul by Muses fed.

Later Years in Florence

O Geist and Kaï ! If we shall meet
Your master midst the fadeless bloom
Of asphodels, so from your tomb
You too shall rise and kiss his feet.

Later she again referred to Matthew Arnold in a pleasant passage :—

"To the philosopher the difference between the human and the other races cannot appear very great, whilst to the poet the solidarity of all sentient life must always seem unquestionable. That friend, and scholar, and poet, for whom I mourn as freshly as though he had died but yesterday, did not disdain to greet a brother's spirit in

'That liquid, melancholy eye
From whose pathetic, soul-fed springs,
Seem'd surging the Virgilian cry,
The sense of tears in mortal things,'

for these lines were written by Matthew Arnold to 'only a dog.'"

Ouida observed that Arnold not only loved his dogs, Geist and Kaï, but he also respected them, "for whoever does not in a fair degree, as with a human friend, respect the freedom, the preference, and the idiosyncrasy of an animal will never reach true comprehension of him." [1]

About this time Ouida's exaggerated feeling for dogs caused division between her and the Cavaliere Tassinari. A mad dog had passed by his villa, and

[1] Cf. *Critical Studies*, "The Quality of Mercy" (1900).

the authorities ordered all the dogs in the commune to be shut up or chained up, a fine of 40 francs to be paid for each dog found loose. Tassinari naturally obeyed, and shut up his dogs in the stable-yard. On hearing this Ouida wrote to his daughter, Mrs. Danyell :—

"I hasten to enclose this for your father. It is horrible to put two great dogs together, and their blood boils till they become unsafe. If he does not let the dogs be free I will cease all friendship for him and consign him to the disgust of posterity as second to the Cenci father in cruelty. If you do not answer me I shall do something."

And from that time Tassinari ceased to exist for her, although, as will be seen, his services and those of his family were always at her disposal in her many difficulties. From another letter [1] we gather still more of her strange methods with dogs.

"Dogs are so very susceptible that no worrying ought to be permitted to them. Pan has just made a wreck of four fine geraniums, and killed them and taken another hat—but I don't touch him. I tell him he is naughty, and he is very repentant—till next time."

She felt also a strong sympathy with the vegetable kingdom, and that feeling and her unreasonable obstinacy caused a quarrel between her and the Marchese Farinola, the landlord of her villa, which ended in her total discomfiture and obliged her to quit

[1] To a member of the Tassinari family.

the house. She sternly refused to have the tall laurel hedges of the old Italian garden clipped and trimmed. The Marchese sent his bailiff to expostulate, and to ask her to keep the park in order. She answered him with, "How would the Marchese like to have his own arms and legs lopped off?" Her obstinacy made the Marchese resolve to cancel his agreement with her and regain possession of the villa. But, not wishing to be discourteous, he asked Sir Dominic Ellis Colnaghi, then British Consul in Florence, to intervene. Colnaghi wrote to Captain Danyell [1]:—

"*June* 3, 1888.

"The day before yesterday the Marchese Farinola called on me with reference to his villa at Scandicci now tenanted by Madame de la Ramé. It appears, if I understand him correctly, that there is some difficulty with regard to the cessation of the tenancy, and before taking any final legal measure the Marchese is anxious that an opportunity of a friendly settlement should not be lost. I said the question was one in which for various reasons I did not see that I could interfere officially, but that I knew a friend of Madame de la Ramé to whom I could write a private line on the subject. . . .

"The landlord requires possession of his villa and intends to take every legal step in his power to obtain it."

[1] Son-in-law of the Cavaliere Tassinari.

Ouida : a Memoir

Ouida, however, refused to listen to reason or to take advice from any quarter, and was consequently submitted to ill-treatment on the part of the gendarmes and peasants sent by the Marchese to force an eviction. Describing what happened, she wrote :—

" They forced the gates, then forced the shutters of the ante-room, which took them two hours, entered so and forced every door in the house, these filthy peasants covering me with abuse."

In the evening the men were withdrawn. Captain Danyell busied himself on Ouida's behalf and went to his friend Senator Gadda, the Prefect of Florence, in the hope of obtaining some redress. On being informed of this Ouida replied : " A thousand thanks. Am waiting for my lawyer. Am a French subject and was presented at the Quirinale by the French Ambassadress." The statement of her French nationality was startling and unexpected. The French Consul, to whom Danyell then appealed, said he would willingly intervene if Ouida would furnish him with documents proving that she was a French subject. Danyell told this to Ouida, who indignantly replied : " What does the Consul mean by establishing facts ? They are established. Unhappily I have no papers of any kind ; my father disappeared after the Commune and his papers with him."

She then went herself to see the Prefect, and her account of the interview is characteristic :—

" I saw Gadda ; he was violent—said I dreamed

things that could occur to no one else ; declared that Farinola could not have been paid.[1] Then he said if he had been, there were the tribunals of the country. I said *quand un gentilhomme* se conduit comme un cuistre, il me semble que les autres gentilhommes du pays doivent le rappeler à raison par l'arrêt d'un tribunal beaucoup plus haut que celui des Cours d'Assizes. He was alarmed and changed his tone and conducted me to the carriage. . . . I fear nothing much can be done until I can go to Rome, but in any event I can always bring an action against the police. There is so much worry and so much injustice in this lovely but unhappy country."

The matter ended, however, in the Marchese's complete victory.

Ouida then went to live in Florence itself, and notwithstanding her lack of means took an apartment of thirty rooms, with a magnificent terrace for the dogs, in the Palazzo Feroni in the Via de Serragli. She still had great and influential friends who were ready to give her substantial pecuniary help. She seemed, however, to have lost all sense of proportion. One morning she wrote a frantic letter to the Marchesa Incontri, who had already lent her large sums, asking for the immediate loan of 500 francs. The Marchesa replied : " I

---

[1] There was a dispute as to whether the rent (3,000 francs) had been paid, Ouida maintaining that it had and the Marchese denying that he had ever received it, and declaring the receipt which was forthcoming after a while to be a forgery.

have not got 500 francs, but I send you 50." The same afternoon Ouida drove up to thank her in a carriage and pair. A rich and influential friend had bought her furniture for 30,000 francs, leaving it, however, in her possession for her own use, while morally, of course, it belonged to him. Following her principle, often enounced, that people with money ought to pay for people with brains, she allowed her creditors to seize it, and it was all sold by auction ; even her manuscripts were hawked about and her most cherished possessions and souvenirs scattered to the winds.

Then began Ouida's painful odyssey from hotel to hotel, from villa to villa. From each she and her dogs would be ignominiously expelled when her bills became too large to allow of further transactions. It is even said that she wandered all one night on the Lung' Arno with her pets. The Tassinari offered her their villa at Signa as a haven of refuge. She answered : "I cannot tolerate people who forget." To one of her most constant friends, who offered her a little villino, Ouida, after viewing the place, answered, although she knew not where to turn at the time, "Woman, do you think I can live in a box ? "

Meanwhile she continued to write to Baron Tauch-nitz, whose son and daughter-in-law had made her personal acquaintance in Florence.

Later Years in Florence

Ouida to Baron Tauchnitz.

"*January* [1889].

" The whole system of English publication is undergoing so great a change, owing to the cheap newspaper Press, that I confess I look forward with apprehension to its future. I very much regret that I did not write my books in my own tongue (French) ; however, I should not in that case have had such pleasant intercourse with your house, so all things have their compensations."

In 1890 she made a new friend in Mrs. H. C. Huntington, who occupied a beautiful villa, the situation of which Ouida greatly admired. Mrs. Huntington remained her firm friend to the last. "I envy you the beautiful old Castellani," Ouida writes, "and that divine sunset view across the plain to Signa and Monte Albano." In September she went to Austria and Venice. The demolition of old buildings and the erection of new ones in Florence were a great trouble to her.

Ouida to Baron Tauchnitz.

"*March* 13 [1891].

" The winter here has been odious and the demolitions of the centre of the city fill the air with putrid dust and germs. Everybody has been ill in some way or another. I am longing to get away either to the Riviera or to Venice."

She had been a constant reader of, and sometimes a contributor to, *The Times*, but she ceased after what she described as the " Parnell-Pigott fiasco." She read and criticized the novels of her contemporaries, and found them dreary and long-winded. But she admired George Meredith's novels and asked Tauchnitz why he did not publish more of them; his reply is interesting.

Baron Tauchnitz to Ouida.

"*May*, 1891.

" We often publish books of which we know they will not have an exterior success, for the reputation of our series, so we tried it with three works of that author, but the sale was too limited, so we were obliged to discontinue the publication."

Ouida had never ceased to admire Lord Lytton, and pursued him with attentions. " I had a breakfast for the Windsors on Saturday and Lord Lytton came —he also spent Sunday with me and will spend to-morrow. He is very delightful," she wrote to Mme. Tassinari. Ouida had paid one visit to Kneb-worth, where she had hoped for a tête-à-tête with its owner. She found, however, to her disappointment that a party was assembled. Among her fellow-guests was Alfred Austin. She wrote a poem in one of her books which she sent him in April, 1891, and in the following years she used often to write to him.

Later Years in Florence

On Lord Lytton's death in 1891 she wrote to Tauchnitz :—

"The death of my beloved friend Lord Lytton makes it impossible for me to attend to anything."

Tauchnitz was issuing a little magazine containing short stories, and asked Ouida if she could suggest some writers of such things.

Ouida to Baron Tauchnitz.

"*September* 24 [1891].

"I can recommend you some stories of Frank Harris in the *Fortnightly Review* ; they are very clever ; as a rule the English cannot write short stories : their construction is too loose and their style too careless."

In 1891 the new Copyright Act, by which the copyright of a book could be secured to the English author and publisher if it was printed in America, was being negotiated. Ouida approved of it and deplored the agitation in the Press, "promoted," as she wrote to Tauchnitz, "by the printers, binders, and paper-makers, who are afraid of their trade going over to America. The interests of the writers of books are always the last considered."

Ouida continued her migrations from villa to villa, and at the same time her requests for advances. At one time she was living at the Villa del Corona, Bellosguardo, which she describes as "a beautiful old place, and was for seven centuries a monastery, until it was secularized by the Great Napoleon," scarcely a residence suited to cramped financial resources. In the spring of 1893 her mother had a bad fall, which resulted in her serious illness and death. Mme. Ramé had throughout worried greatly over their financial difficulties, and was not in a condition to throw off the effects of the accident. On August 2nd, Ouida asks Tauchnitz for an advance and tells him : "If I do not pay my rent for this villa[1] on the eighth I shall be turned out of it. . . . My mother has had a bad fall and is very ill, and if she had to leave the house it would kill her."

Tauchnitz replied five days later, sending Ouida a sum of money, and, commenting on the fact that he had received no book of hers for some time, told her that " our readers much miss your famous pen in our series."

Ouida to Baron Tauchnitz.

" *August* 11 [1893].

" I am most grateful for your kind response to my request. . . . The house laws are most harsh and entirely in the landlord's favour."

" *August* 30 [1893].

" My mother has been in a condition in which she might die at any moment. . . . This prolonged illness of my mother's (four months) has crippled me terribly."

[1] Probably the Villa la Campora, Bellosguardo.

MADAME RAMÉ : OUIDA'S MOTHER.

From a photograph.

To face p. 146.

Later Years in Florence

" September 9, 1893.

" It is a most costly and cruel illness."

" September 10, 1893.

"She is dead."

" September 24 [1893].

" I thank you infinitely for your kind sympathy, and for the practical aid which you gave me during a period of unspeakable suffering, both physical and mental. I shall never forget the goodness of you and of your son. You are a real friend ; the world holds but few."

"November 8 [1893].

" I cannot tell you how I miss my mother, nor how I am haunted by the remembrance of all her great sufferings after her fall. Her eyes were so beautiful to the last, and like those of a woman of twenty. Her little dog Rex is still very unhappy, though none of his habits are changed, and he is fond of me."

So crippled were Ouida's resources that her mother was actually buried in the pauper's portion of the Allori Cemetery at Florence. It seems incredible that this need have been, and it is quite certain that had they known the exact condition of things Ouida's friends would have prevented it, but her foolish pride stood in the way.

Mme. Ramé's death was a great blow to Ouida. She would have fully endorsed Gray's remark on a similar

147

occasion, "We can only have one single mother." The mother and daughter had only been separated two or three times in the fifty-three years since Ouida's birth. Ouida never ceased to miss her mother's adoring affection and admiration. Writing to Alfred Austin some time after the sad event, she said : "I shall miss her as long as I live, and if the knowledge that all are dead who cared for me be bracing, I have that tonic."

To another correspondent,[1] she wrote several years later :—

"I am so sorry you have lost your mother. It is a loss one feels more, not less, with each succeeding year. I lost mine five years ago. She gave me the happiest childhood ever led on earth ; and I know now that I was always utterly ungrateful. A Florentine peasant said once to me : 'Whilst one's mother lives one is never old, for there is always some one for whom one is young.'"

Rex, the little Maltese terrier that belonged to Mme. Ramé, was inconsolable at her death. He refused all food for three weeks, and was kept alive by nourishment artificially administered. He sat up and begged day after day before her bed and before her favourite chair, until he dropped from sheer exhaustion. Whenever the door opened he thought she entered. He ran and looked into every stranger's face. He knew everything which had belonged to her. His sorrow injured

[1] Mr. Sydney C. Cockerell, see p. 172.

his health ; his heart became weak, and he died of cardiac paralysis at six years old. Ouida, in relating this fact, asks, " What could human affection offer superior in fidelity and feeling ? "

Ouida's loneliness was naturally increased by the loss of her mother, and as a consequence the obstinacy, unreasonableness, and foolish pride that had already marked Ouida's actions were intensified, and as time progressed it became more and more difficult to give her the assistance which, to the credit of all concerned, be it said, was always forthcoming. She would tear up and then return the cheques sent her, and when a kind friend arranged that meals should be provided her from one of the best restaurants in Florence, Ouida gave the food to the dogs, that they might enjoy their meals and feel no want, and continued herself to live on tea and biscuits. " I am weary of everything," she wrote, " except my dogs."

In 1894 Ouida left Florence for Lucca. She never again visited Florence.

In the period 1880 to 1889, Ouida produced thirteen works, including long novels and volumes of short stories, and dramatic sketches. Of the longer books, *In Maremma* (1882) is certainly the best, *A Village Commune* (1881) inaugurates the stories that deal with the woes of the Italian peasantry, *Wanda* (1883) is on the lines of the novels of the seventies, and in its setting and some of its characteristics recalls *Idalia*, while in *Moths* (1880), *Princess Napraxine* (1884), and its sequel, *Othmar* (1885) Ouida develops a new type of heroine, a sort of Undine of fashionable life, who only finds her soul after destroying those of many other people. In *Guilderoy* (1889) some people chose to see a fancy portrait of Lord Lytton. Ouida herself, in a letter to Lady Dorothy Nevill (January 12, 1888), described it as "a very harmless novel, very Conservative, and containing a eulogy of Lord Salisbury." She had been greatly irritated at the delayed publication of this novel—it had been finished and paid for in 1886—and even thought that the publishers had received a large sum of money to suppress it altogether.[1] *A House Party* (1887) was the outcome of a play she had tried and failed to write for the Bancrofts. One of the volumes of short stories, *Bimbi* (1882), contains four delightful tales for children, though none of them equals in charm and pathos *A Dog of Flanders*, published ten years earlier.

Between 1890 and 1894, years, as we have seen, of great stress, Ouida wrote only a few short stories and magazine articles. Some of the latter were afterwards reprinted.[2] The most notable was perhaps a violent diatribe against vivisection entitled *The New Priesthood*.[3]

---

[1] Cf. Lady Dorothy Nevill, *Under Five Reigns* (1910), Chap. viii.
[2] Cf. *Views and Opinions* (1895) ; cf. Chap. viii.
[3] Reprinted in *Toxin and Other Papers* (Tauchnitz, 1896).

V

LUCCA
1894—1903

CHAPTER V

LUCCA

1894–1903

OUIDA left Florence in a very depressed state of mind. She chose Lucca as a place of refuge in her troubles, not because she liked the city, but because under the circumstances it offered certain advantages. Soon after her arrival she wrote to Mrs. Huntington :—

"I *don't* like Lucca. . . . I don't think I shall ever like anything ever again. . . . I should not like to live and die here ; it does not seem Italy at all, and one never sees a flower."

She did not stay very long in Lucca itself. By June she had moved to Sant' Alessio, three miles from Lucca, where she took a villa for the summer. Her letters refer to lack of money and reveal her general distress. For three or four months after leaving Florence she did not write to Tauchnitz.

Ouida to Baron Tauchnitz.

"LUCCA, *per* S. ALESSIO,
"*June* 20, 1894.

"I have had great misfortunes since I wrote to you, personal and financial, which occupied my mind too

153

painfully to leave me thought for correspondence. I have been two months at the sea, which did me good, and now have taken this villa for the summer. It is very beautiful."

From now onwards Ouida's letters to Tauchnitz contain references to her financial difficulties :—

"S. Alessio, Lucca,
"*June* 30 [1894].

" I am at this moment utterly impoverished by the infamies of my men of business. . . . In a few months my fortunes will mend."

" *December* 9 [1894 ?].

" I have had very heavy losses, due to dishonest lawyers and absconding bankers, but the tide has now turned and the worst is passed. Many people in Florence lost everything in the krach ; five banks went down in a single year."

At this period Ouida was writing only short stories, many of which were published in the *Illustrated London News* and the *Sketch* under the editorship of Mr. Clement Shorter. Her offer to illustrate them herself was declined. She could still command a certain public, but English readers have never taken kindly to volumes of short stories, and thus, while she had no long novel to offer, it was not an easy matter to find publishers. It was about this time that her connection with Mr. T. Fisher Unwin, to whom this memoir owes its being, began. Ouida was drawn to him not only in the way of business, but also through his well-known sympathy with many of the causes that she had at heart. In addition, his political views coincided with hers, as we shall see later, in the South African War and in the estimate of Joseph Chamberlain.

In June, 1894, Mr. Unwin published *The Silver Christ* in his "Pseudonym Library"; *Toxin* appeared in the same series in October, 1895. Some discussion arose between author and publisher as to the length of those stories, and Ouida wrote :—

"The B.P. is not brilliant, but I cannot believe it is so imbecile as to buy books only by their length."

While the negotiations concerning *Toxin* were proceeding, Ouida drew the publisher's attention to her conditions of work :—

Ouida to T. Fisher Unwin.

"*September* 16, 1894.

"I never state name, place, or story of any novel before it is purchased. I have never done so. I have always received the entire money down before giving the MS. Indeed, I have frequently received it before the work was written."

Ouida : a Memoir

In December Mr. Unwin sent her some reviews of her stories, which she thus acknowledged :—

"You have sent me a number of foolish extracts, miscalled reviews. They are not worth the postage. They are for the most part the envious yapping of 'those who have failed in literature and art.'"

In 1895 she published with Mr. Methuen a collection of essays she had contributed to various periodicals, under the title of *Views and Opinions.* The essays showed that Ouida possessed critical power of no low degree.

Her letters this year are greatly occupied with her publishing difficulties. The royalty system had become the rule, and to it she strongly objected.

By January, 1895, she was settled in the Villa Massoni at Sant' Alessio, which became her home until November, 1903. Its fine gardens had particularly tempted her, as they reminded her of those of the Villa Farinola. The trees were even finer, but it was very solitary, and in later years she wrote to Mrs. Huntington that perhaps it had been a mistake, as it isolated her from society.

"It is a paradise for dogs, and very good for writing and reading, as it is wholly out of the world. There is a very pretty view of the little city across the woods."

She found the climate better than that of Florence on the whole, as the cold, biting wind was absent, but the sun was less bright. Of course, it goes without saying that in the precarious state of her

OUIDA IN 1896.

From a chalk drawing by Sarmento in the possession of the artist.

To face p. 157.

finances Ouida acted most unwisely in again taking a large house. She seems to have managed to pay the rent, but fell into debt for everything besides.

The isolation weighed on her at times, and shows itself in her letters.

Ouida to Baron Tauchnitz.

"S. ALESSIO, LUCCA
[*March* 8, 1896].

" The loss of one's mother [1] is so dreadful, cutting down a love which has been our mainstay ever since we can remember. I assure you my regret for my own grows greater every day."

[*September* 16, 1896.]

" This place is very lovely ; it is three miles from Lucca, with very fine trees, and gets the sea scent and sea breeze. But it is quite out of the world—my world. Perhaps so much the better."

She continued to follow with interest all that was going on in the world, though actually she saw very few people.

Ouida to Mrs. Huntington.

" LUCCA,
" *April* 17 [1896].

" I knew Oscar Wilde very well ; he sent me *Dorian Grey*, and I *did* understand it ; I do not think he is a clever man ; he was a successful poseur

[1] Baron Tauchnitz had just lost his mother.

and plagiarist ; he was essentially the *cabotin*. 'I have written three comedies in one year,' he said to a friend of mine, and my friend replied : 'A great exercise of memory!' The Italian papers assign him a much higher place than that which he held in London society. I am most grieved for his mother, a talented and devoted woman who has had nothing but sorrow all her life. It may be very immoral of me, but I do not think the law should meddle with these offences. The publicity caused does much more harm than the offence itself."

Ouida to Baron Tauchnitz.

[*October* 13, 1896.]

"Poor Du Maurier! Death is always mal-àpropos, and takes those to whom life is worth most."

"*October* 19 [1896].

"I think *Trilby* was made by the Press partly, and partly by its *brio* and freshness. The first volume is charming. The second I think is rubbish. *I* liked his *Peter Ibbetson*, which most found tiresome."

Again and again a note of depression is sounded, and in January, 1897, she writes :—

"One clings to old friendships and old memories as the sun of life sinks lower."

In 1897 she published *The Massarenes*, the first long novel she had issued for some years. Tauchnitz had informed her that the sale of her books was falling off, and when she expressed to him her doubts, he gave her, in an interesting letter, what he thought were the probable reasons.

Baron Tauchnitz to Ouida.

"LEIPZIG,
"*March* 23, 1897.

" I rather thought of the general state of things on the market of English literature, amongst which I might point out the *enormous over-production* and the *wonderfully varying* taste of the public. As to the over-production, I do whatever is in my power to limit it on the Continent ; against the taste of the public I am quite powerless. You know best yourself that real merits and popularity in literature are sometimes together, but unfortunately sometimes not, and there is many a riddle which we publishers cannot explain, in spite of the longest experience."

The publication of *The Massarenes* seems to have afforded Ouida some temporary pecuniary relief.

Ouida to Baron Tauchnitz.

"LUCCA,
" *March* 27, 1897.

" I think you will find *The Massarenes* worth ten thousand *Trilbys.*[1] But it will be certainly extremely unpopular.

[1] Tauchnitz told her in a previous letter that *Trilby* had had the biggest sale of any novel in his series for many years.

Ouida : a Memoir

" . . . Look at the poverty of the best English reviews. Compare them with the *R. d. D. Mondes* or the *Revue de Paris*. I had to wait six months for the *Fortnightly* to screw up its courage to publish my *d'Annunzio* in this month's number. . . ."

Ouida herself set great store by *The Massarenes* and was delighted at its success.

Ouida to Baron Tauchnitz.

"*April* 12, 1897.

" Are you reading *The Massarenes*? Of course the English Press loathes it, belonging, as that Press does, to the ' richards,' and in some instances to new peers. I can assure you it is not a whit overdrawn."

"*April* 25 [1897].

" *The Massarenes* makes a great impression and sells largely. . . . It is impossible to exaggerate the greed of English society. I saw with my own eyes their *rush* for the Mackays. . . .

" There is not an iota of exaggeration in my book, and I am thankful I have lived to show them themselves as they are. The Englishman of our old ideal is dead—or nearly so. . . .

" I would not say the whole of English society is thus, but the whole of what we call ' *smart* society ' (which used to be called ' *high* ' society) is so. . . . The book is brassé dans le vrai.

" Don't you think it is worth many *Trilbys* ? "

Lucca

The book is an overdrawn, lurid picture of the vices, manners, and customs of the so-called "smart set" of the period, and of the entry into it of the American millionaire, who is received solely by reason of his wealth. According to Ouida, in the set she describes no woman is virtuous, no man's children are his own; her personages are either monsters of vice or impossible perfections of virtue. A Royal personage easily to be distinguished is shown in a very unpleasant light. Yet with it all the book is not ill-constructed, and the character of the wicked heroine neither wholly inconsistent nor wholly inconceivable. Ouida declared that ten years ago Mudie would have refused to circulate it, and that it was thought "ripping good fun" by London society.

The rejoicings in England for Queen Victoria's Diamond Jubilee roused all Ouida's ire. An article expressing a similar view to her own appeared in the journal of the Humanitarian League, a society in which, as will be seen, Ouida was greatly interested. It was written by Henry S. Salt, the Hon. Secretary of the Association, and after reading it Ouida wrote to him :—

"17 *July* [1897].

" I write to you myself to express my full sympathy with your Jubilee views. It has been the apotheosis of Philistia, and was, I think, a crime as well as a vulgarity, at a moment when famine and plague tortured India. And with all this bombast

England could not stand against the Franco-Russian-German-Turkish coalition, which is quite on the cards, against her. She is only civil to Italy, who, in such an event, neither could or would do anything to assist her.

" . . . . I have not touched Vegetarianism, [1] and I fear it will never become general. I wish we could live by smelling flowers, like the happy people in La Fontaine's story."

This year Ouida published also a story called *The Altruist*, intended to show how impossible it was for a man of rank and wealth to live in accordance with the socialistic views he had adopted.

Ouida to Baron Tauchnitz.

[*October* 28, 1897.]

" I hear Lord Salisbury says *The Altruist* is the cleverest thing that has been written for ages. I cannot return the compliment as to his foreign policy, for never was any policy more fatal, at once weak and inflammatory, and the ' Concert ' as to Crete is grotesque. The Sultan jockeys them all.

" Would you kindly send me *The Martians*? There is a dear big dog in it, I see."

Finding that she could not always easily dispose of

---

[1] Mr. Salt had asked for an article from her on that subject for his paper.

her short stories and that even for long novels, had she any on the stocks, protracted negotiations were now required, Ouida turned her attention to criticism, both literary and political, and began to write for the serious reviews, chiefly for the *Fortnightly*, the *Nineteenth Century*, and the *North American Review*. In March, 1897, appeared an article by her in the *Fortnightly* on "Gabriele d' Annunzio," the first ever printed in English on that writer. It is an admirable piece of criticism, and I shall endeavour to show in a later chapter the fine qualities of Ouida's critical power. It was followed in September by an article on "Georges Darien," the author of novels on the subject of the Franco-German War of 1870–71 and all its horrors. She also contributed articles in Italian to the *Nuova Antologia*, which she afterwards translated into English herself. Some of those dealt with the condition of Italy, of course, as Ouida saw it.

In answer to a request from Mr. W. H. Stead, she wrote at the time of the Milan riots (April—May, 1898) an article in the *Review of Reviews* entitled "An Impeachment of Modern Italy" which is a scathing indictment of the Italian methods of government.

The editor of the *Nineteenth Century* asked Ouida to write for him an article on "The Italian Novels of Marion Crawford." She complied, and it appeared in October, 1898. The article is more interesting perhaps for the light it throws on Ouida's own attitude to and knowledge of Italy than for its criticism of the novelist. Take the following passages, for example :—

"In Italy he [1] lives only for the people around him as he would live in Pall Mall, or Broadway, or the Champs Elysées. That passion with which Italy has inspired Shelley, Byron, George Sand, De Musset, Owen Meredith, even the calm analytic mind of Taine, has never touched him. He has never felt the ecstasy which is embodied in that single phrase of Taine's, ' *On nage dans la lumière.*' One would say that the moonlight shining on the waters of Tiber, under the bridge of St. Angelo, is no more to him than a flash-light illumining a grain elevator on the Hudson. All which is still Italy, of colour, of perfume, of light, of legend, of rapture, of emotion, has wholly escaped him ; he has never felt its *hysterica passio* ; he has never known its eternal youth, he has never seen its lost gods rise and walk through its blossoming grass as the star rays shine in the white cups of the narcissus of its fields."

Again, Ouida combats from her own experience Crawford's statement that the Italians have no imagination :—

"This is but partially true ; I am not sure that it is true at all. Their modern poetry is beautiful, more beautiful than that of any other nation. Their popular songs are poetic and impassioned as those of no other nation are, and one may hear among their

[1] Crawford.

peasantry expressions of singular beauty of sentiment and phrase. A woman of middle age, a *contadina*,
said to me once, 'So long as one's mother lives, one's
youth is never quite gone, for there is always some-
body for whom one is young.' A rough, rude man,
a day-labourer, who knew not a letter and spent all
his life bent over his spade or plough, said to me
once, one lovely night in spring, as he looked up at
the full moon, 'How beautiful she is! But she has
no heart. She sees us toiling and groaning and
suffering down here, and she is always fair and calm,
and never weeps!' Another said once, when a tree
was hard to fell, 'He is sorry to come away, it has
been his field so long.' And when a flock of solan
geese flew over our lands, going from the marches to
the mountains on their homeward way, and descended
to rest, the peasants did not touch them: 'They are
tired, poor souls,' said one of the women; 'one
must not grudge them the soil for their lodging.'
Surely such ideas as these in people wholly uneducated
indicate imagination in the speakers?"

Crawford, however, was as outspoken in his
criticism of things Italian as Ouida was, and perhaps
more so.

Ouida to Baron Tauchnitz.

"*February* 26 [1899].

"I hear Crawford is banished from Court in Rome
because the Queen is so angry at what he said about

the Quirinal, etc. She would be wiser to reflect
that when two persons so unlike each other as Crawford and I both condemn a regime, there must be
grave faults in it. But Royal people put their heads
in a sack and never see daylight."

Ouida watched the Dreyfus case with great interest.

Ouida to Baron Tauchnitz.

[*August*, 1899.]

" I am deeply anxious about the Dreyfus affair ;—
not for the man, of whose guilt I am convinced—but
lest it should bring on war between France and
Germany."

In December, 1899, Ouida published in Italian, in
the *Nuova Antologia*, a scathing article on Chamberlain, a translation of which, as we shall see, was later
published in her *Critical Studies*.[1]

Ouida to Baron Tauchnitz.

"*December* 31, 1899.

" I must send you a word of greeting and also of
memory at the close of this century, in which I have
received so many acts of kindness and friendship from
your father and from you. I think you know how
deeply I have felt these.

" You do not read Italian, or I would send you an

[1] Unwin, 1900.

article of mine against Chamberlain in the *Nuova Antologia* which has made some stir.

" Pray accept my warmest wishes for your happiness and prosperity."

In the spring of 1900 Mr. Wilfrid Scawen Blunt stopped at Pisa, and with Mr. Sydney C. Cockerell, who was travelling with him, paid Ouida a visit at Sant' Alessio. Ouida had already corresponded with Mr. Blunt, and had published an article on him and his works, reprinted in *Critical Studies*. There she says of him [1] :—

" There are few men of our time more interesting than the man who bears this name. Fresh with English air and dark with desert suns, passionately liberal in thought and nobly independent in opinion, spending his winters on the shores of the Nile, on the edge of the desert, and his summers between the vale of Shoreham and the alder-shaded water of the humble Mole, he touches, and has always touched, life at its most different facets.

" His private life, likewise, is equally of interest to the most indifferent, since he is the husband of Byron's granddaughter, the father-in-law of Neville Lytton, the companion in youth of Owen Meredith, the friend of the Arab, the champion of the dumb, and the standard-bearer of all lost causes."

Mr. Blunt has kindly contributed to this volume

[1] Cf. *Critical Studies* (1900).

some extracts from Ouida's letters to him, a most interesting account from his diary of the visit of April, 1900, as well as his estimate of her as a novelist,[1] and as a worker in the cause of humanity.[2]

The following extracts are from letters written to Mr. Blunt before their meeting.

Ouida to Wilfrid Scawen Blunt.

" *November* 30, 1899.

" Words, however powerful, utterly fail to turn the tide of the sort of brutal insanity which is now possessing the English nation. I fear that for many thousands of years Africa will be a field of battle. The powers who hate each other are there cheek by jowl, like live snakes shut up in a basket, and the natives will always suffer as long as they are allowed to live. I am extremely anxious as to France ; she is completely isolated and, if Chamberlain continues the leader of England, he will 'go for' Madagascar before very long. I have written an article on him in the *Nuova Antologia* of the 1st December. What do the Philistines say to your poem and the magnificent indictment by Satan ? Matthew Arnold would have understood and appreciated it. I thank you for the courageous words of the preface and the supreme truths of Satan's reproach. What you say of the Anglo-Saxon race is absolutely true, and I myself have drawn down on me bitter enmity by saying similar things."

[1] See pp. 273–4.   [2] See p. 327.

Lucca

"I do the little I can to make the nation recover its sanity, but it seems a hopeless task. Chamberlain has bought all the London Press except the *W. G.*, the *Star*, and the *Morning Leader*; and the war party sends lecturers to rouse even remote little provincial towns with the most horrible stories of the 'atrocities' of the Boers. It makes one think of the Bulgarian atrocities, when 'the impaled Christians' turned out to be posts of wood to mark the height of the river. You do not say anything of Egypt; but surely it would be a favourable moment for the Egyptians to turn out the English. Do say something of these tortured lions.[1] It is so frightful to degrade the desert majesty thus, and surely it is a most demoralizing spectacle for the public. I have heard that their subjection is obtained by means of unmentionable cruelties. Something certainly most frightful must be done to them. I assure you the cruelty of the world makes me miserable, and it appears to me a thousand times worse than twenty years ago. How can we hope that such a world will see the beauty and truth of your Satan?"

The account of the visit to Sant' Alessio, taken from Mr. Blunt's diary of the time, is as follows :—

" *April* 21, 1900.

" We went, Cockerell and I, to call on Ouida at her villa at S. Alessio. Our driver did not know the

---

[1] Probably an allusion to beasts kept in menageries.

house or understand who it was that we wanted to visit, but at last suggested, in answer to our questions, 'The lady with the many dogs.' 'Oh yes,' we said, 'the lady with the dogs.' And so, sure enough, it was. Arrived there, we found it to be a nice old villa, with trees and a high garden wall and an eighteenth-century iron gate, towards which, from inside, seven or eight dogs, poodles and nondescripts, came at us openmouthed. The noise was deafening, and it was some time before we could make our ringing heard. At last the bell was answered by a portly man-cook in cap and apron, who, after some delay consequent on my sending in my card, admitted us. At the end of ten minutes we were shown into a front hall, and there found the lady of the house, seated at a small table (as one finds in the opening scene of a play)—a little old lady, dressed in white, who rose to meet us and to reprove her dogs, who were yelping at us still in chorus. A mild reproof it was, nor did it save us from their caresses. The largest poodle placed his paws upon my knees, and another took my hat in his mouth. 'They do not often bite,' she explained, 'except beggars.'

" We sat down and talked. I had been prepared, by the violence of some of her writings and by what I had just heard of her,[1] to find her somewhat loud and masculine ; but she proved the reverse of this. In

---

[1] Mr. Blunt had just been in Florence, and had heard the tales current there about Ouida.

Lucca

face Ouida is much more French than English; her father, she told us, was French, M. Ramé, and her mother an Englishwoman. She is small-featured, soft and distinguished, though she can never have been pretty, with a high forehead, rather prominent blue eyes, dulled and watery with age, almost white hair, and that milk-and-roses complexion which old people sometimes get, and which gives them a beatified look. It was difficult to understand her capable of such a malevolence as her *Friendship*. She can never, I think, have been a sensual woman or have inspired a sensual affection, whatever passions she may display in her writings. Her conversation is good, intellectual, but not affected or the talk of a blue-stocking; it gives one the impression of a woman who has thought out her ideas and has the courage still of her opinions. We talked about the inhumanity of modern Europe, and especially of modern England, and the rage for slaughter which is its chief feature. We talked also about Italy and Crispi, who is her *bête noire* here, as Chamberlain is in England. She talks English perfectly, as she says she does also French and Italian, and she complained to us of the slip-shod writing of the day. It was evidently a pleasure to her to talk and to find us such good listeners. She was greatly taken with Cockerell, perhaps for his modesty, and was curious as to who he could be, for I had not introduced him. 'Who is he?' she said to me in private, 'who is he *really*'?"

Ouida : a Memoir

"When at the end of a couple of hours we moved to go, she would have detained us and made us both promise to come again. She cannot go now to England on her dogs' account, for these monopolize her life. Altogether she is a somewhat pathetic figure, condemned to solitude, not by choice but by necessity, and regretting the cheerful society of Florence. The exile from it has, I fancy, been the work of her books, for she has had a bitter pen. 'The world takes its revenge on us,' she said, 'for having despised it.' We both left her with feelings of respect, almost of affection, certainly of sympathy."

They neither of them found an opportunity of repeating their visit, but both maintained a correspondence with her until near the day of her death.

The visit was a source of great satisfaction to Ouida. Writing to Mr. Blunt on April 24, she said : "I cannot tell you the great pleasure your visit gave me. . . . I should be in England this summer probably, were it not for the dog laws of the worst Government the century has seen. . . . When you write, tell me a little about your companion.[1] I thought him delightful."

A long and fairly regular correspondence ensued between Ouida and Mr. Cockerell, her last letter to him being written, as will be seen, only a week before her death. Mr. Cockerell has most kindly permitted me to make extracts from the letters, and his co-

[1] Mr. Sydney C. Cockerell.

172

operation is of the greatest value to this memoir.
For Ouida's letters to him show in many ways the
best of her serious "soul-side." Due, perhaps, to the
oncoming of age or to certain teachings of experience,
or may be to the good influence of the temperament
of her correspondent—for when we wish to stand well
with a person, because we like and esteem him, we
are sure to be at our best—there is, in these letters,
less of the personal vanity that mars so many of her
utterances. Their tone is often very serious, and they
reveal in some ways her attitude to the great problems
of life and to the pressing questions of the day. Many
of her opinions are, however, as usual, couched in
vehement language, and some of her remarks on
persons ill-considered and extravagant.

Ouida was greatly exercised about the Boer War,
and in speech and writing frankly declared herself
Pro-Boer throughout ; most of her letters written
during 1900 and 1901 contain observations on the
war very strongly expressed. She always insisted
on calling it a financiers' war. Curiously enough, in
1891 a mining company at Kimberley had named
itself the "Ouida Prospecting Syndicate" ; its
promoters doubtless imagined they were paying a
welcome compliment to the authoress. She, however,
took a different view, and wrote to *The Times*[1] to say
that she had nothing to do with it, and continued :
" I consider the appropriation of my name the greatest

[1] Her letter appeared on March 6, 1891.

impertinence. . . . I abhor the greedy and shameless parcelling out of Africa by a mob of European speculators."

Ouida to Baron Tauchnitz.

"*January* 18 [1900].

"The [book] trade is suffering from this vile war. The English nation seems quite insane, and I think it would be well if Europe gave it a lesson."

January 30 [1900].

"How disgraceful is the state of politics, Press, and public opinion in the British nation! It amazes me."

[*February*, 1900.]

"The war kills all reasonable things and all impersonal interests. The English nation is mad pro tem."

[*February*, 1900.]

"English Literature as a whole has fallen low of late years. . . .

"I have been writing a good deal politically of late, both in Italian and English. It is a frightful thing that this war should be carried on solely to suit the manœuvres of Chamberlain, Rhodes, and the Stock Exchange. Europe should have intervened last August.

"PS. I just see in your catalogue that you append another name to Ouida.[1] Please take it out. I have

---

[1] Louise de la Ramé.

no other name in Literature. And it should not be put in inverted commas."

" *March* 2, 1900.

"Many thanks. It is of no great consequence, but it is always a pity to confuse the public with two names. Besides, I *love* ' Ouida.' It is my *very own*, as the children say. I don't care for any other of the names I bear."

To Mr. Fisher Unwin Ouida wrote frequently during this period. He had published her *Waters of Edera*. Mr. G. K. Chesterton was then acting as his reader, and his report on it is amusing, for it is characteristic of the writer [1] and also contains pertinent criticism of Ouida's methods :—

"This is, of course, a picturesque, animated, poetic, eloquent, and supremely nonsensical story : it is by Ouida : and age does not wither nor custom stale her infinite lack of variety. Here we have the old division of humanity into a vast majority of brutal and brainless modern people and a small minority of beautiful peasants and beautiful patricians. The story is really fascinating in its description of the Italian country-folk : those of them that are not too pedantically pagan. It is the story of a peasant who apparently owned the whole of a river (which strikes us as improbable), and whose river the detestable Govern-

---

[1] It is printed here by permission of Mr. G. K. Chesterton and Mr. Unwin. It was written in 1899.

ment of modern Italy diverted from its course, wholly regardless of the fact that the peasant in question 'looked like a picture by Giorgione.'

" Then there is an old priest, a scholar and a gentleman, who goes to Rome to point out this pictorial resemblance, and any other arguments he may have, to the execrable Government, and who comes back well primed up in his ' Ouida ' to inform the peasant that there is now no God but gold, and that all modern civilization is going down hill with a rush. But though it is impossible not to smile at Ouida, it is equally impossible not to read her. Whatever the peasant may have been, she is really like an early Italian picture. In the gorgeous and symbolic colouring, intoxicating to the eyes, we forget the silliness of the subjects and the absurdity of the human anatomy."

Ouida sent a copy of the book to her friend Sarmento.

Ouida to Sarmento.

" *March* 6 [1900].

" You are first amongst the few people whose appreciations of a work of mine are delightful to me because they are so intelligent and select the true qualities which merit most praise and sympathy. I always told you that you had the making in you of a great critic ; a second Ste.-Beuve. I desired to make the story as realistic as possible. It was suggested to me by a precious scheme now before the Camera to turn aside and use for such works a beautiful tumbling stream called the [Brembo] above Brescia.

"The dreadful project to make a tramway from Mestre and so through Venice is, I fear, likely to be carried, though there is not the slightest need for it. Just now I can think of nothing but of the disasters of the brave Boers and the disgusting drunken vileness of the English nation.

"I am sorry not to have been in Rome. I get *stucca*[1] here, and to my horror they are cutting down all the woods above here, so that the sole charm of the place will by summer be gone. En vérité je n'ai pas de chance."

"*April* 3 [1900].

"I shall indeed be glad if you come to V.[2] It seems years since I saw you and there are things I should like to ask you about. We can then speak, too, of your writing criticisms for the Press. I should love to see a journal of criticism without fear or favour. All those existing are worthless.

"I cannot agree that Rostand is a genius or even a poet. He is obnoxious to me with his jeweller's similes. When the Duc de Reichstadt is asked what he would go first to see in Paris, he says the Vendôme Column! Look at this :—

> "'Le bon St. Pierre ôtant son auréole d'or
> Pour ne pas être trahi par ses feux. . . .'

[1] Weary.　　　　[2] Viareggio.

He writes dramatically for the stage, and he has enormous réclame ; but he is no poet."

Ouida's opinion of her own merits did not decrease as she grew older. The letter of which we print a facsimile was written to Mr. Unwin in 1900. She also told him that she had refused several offers for the translation of *The Massarenes*, "as I am convinced it is untranslatable, except by myself, and I cannot take the trouble."

In other letters to the same correspondent she characterized Mrs. Craigie's plays as "very poor stuff; there is no plot at all and the little action there is, wholly improbable."

About this time, too, she received a letter from a newspaper syndicate offering her £24 for two stories. She endorsed it: "What impudence! Of course I shall not answer." Similarly, when in February, 1899, an offer had been made her for a Christmas story, she wrote to Mr. Unwin :—

"I do not write Christmas stories, *i.e.*, tales glorifying that epoch of slaughter and gluttony."

She now began to discuss with Mr. Unwin the question of collecting the articles she had written in the various Reviews and publishing them in volume form.

Ouida to T. Fisher Unwin.

"*March* 17, 1900.

"I had forgotten the essays. Let us issue them ; I will add to those you have—a short one on Auberon

My dear Sir

Pray do not bracket any books of mine with others there. My works are some thing more than Novels of a season. If not, I have lived in vain.

Sincerely yr

Ouida

Saturday

FACSIMILE OF LETTER TO T. FISHER UNWIN.

To face p. 178.

Herbert; the *Unwritten Literary Laws*; and my
Chamberlain of the *Nuova Antologia*. I wrote it in
Italian, but will put it into English myself."

She made it quite clear that she thought highly
of the essays, and declared that she did not desire to
re-issue them for the sake of payment, but "to preserve
work which has in it much thought which is, I venture
to say, worthy of preservation; and this is more than
can be said of ninety-nine out of every hundred
volumes published in London; for English literature
was never at a lower level."

Ouida desired to print in the volume an English
translation of her article on Chamberlain published in the *Nuova Antologia* for December, 1899.[1]
It was, however, of so personal and vehement a nature
that there was some doubt as to the advisability of
issuing it in England. Eventually it was decided
that, as the article appeared in the nature of fair
criticism of a public man, it should be included in
the volume.

The book contained thirteen essays reprinted from
the *Fortnightly*, the *Nineteenth Century*, and the *Nuova
Antologia*: those that had appeared in the last Ouida
herself translated into English. The essays dealt with
a variety of subjects: with books and literature,

[1] Ouida was most anxious that friends in England should read
the article, and on May 27, 1900, wrote to Mr. Cockerell: "Tell
me, when you write, if you read Italian. Frederic Harrison is the
only Englishman I know who does."

English, French, and Italian; with men and matters, political and social; with art; with the woes of animals. Their critical value will be dealt with in a later chapter. The book had success. Published in August, it was reprinted in September and November. Ouida wrote to Mr. Unwin in September :—

"Keep my book at the *head* of your advertisement lists. You have nothing to equal it."

And again :—

"You should not put author of anything on the title-page when the writer is well-known."

Ouida sent the volume to Mr. Cockerell, and his appreciation greatly pleased her and gave her opportunity for emphatic assertion of the sincerity of her views.

Ouida to Sydney C. Cockerell.

"*August* 18 [1900].

"Your letter gave me great pleasure. It is delightful to be understood. Do you think 'Joe' will read what I say?—I fear not. . . .

"It does demand a certain courage to go against the current of the time; and it makes one lose both friends and money; and the Jingo Press is a bad enemy; but oh! the supreme joy of saying the truth as one sees it! and if there be a duty on earth it is this. I have never in my life written a word which I did not entirely believe. . . .

Lucca

"I don't think anything would turn the tide of British swagger YET. Those people who do see, and can keep their heads, are too silent."

In October, 1900, Ouida sent some verses entitled "The Brass Orchid" to the *Speaker*, asking the editor if he did not see fit to publish them to send them on to Mr. Cockerell. They were violently abusive of Chamberlain and wholly unsuited for publication in the Press of Great Britain. The first stanza runs :—

> "O red red Rose of England! Hide your head.
> The Duke of Birmingham commands, instead
> A metal orchid, as the emblem meet
> Of Britain kneeling at great Joseph's feet." [1]

She continued her diatribes against things in general in her letters to her friends.

Ouida to Sydney C. Cockerell.

"*November* 17, 1900.

"I love Morris's [2] eloquence, but in his remedies I cannot believe. The *plebs* will never be much better than they are as regards taste and light. Their life would be unendurable to them if they saw it as it is ;

---

[1] At the head were these words quoted from the *Morning Post* :—"Mr. Chamberlain's supporters have a new badge ; they wear a metal orchid in their buttonholes, as symbol of their political chief and creed."

[2] *I.e.*, William Morris.

and the sweaters' victims are worse off than were the slaves of Imperial Rome."

" December 19, 1900.

" What a spectacle the two Houses at Westminster give to Europe ! Was it utterly impossible for Lord Salisbury to find men whose hands were clean ? I am told that the Opposition dare not attack Joe on account of the tripotages of Asquith and Campbell-Bannerman.

" I had a very pleasant and sympathetic letter from Curzon. He is doing all he can to preserve the architecture of Hindostan ; the destruction there in the last century has been unspeakably ruinous. The English have behaved there just as modern Italians do here."

Ouida to T. Fisher Unwin.

[1900.]

" Alas ! the few who are sane like ourselves on English matters are a very small minority. The Parliamentary Opposition has let slip a fine opportunity and is miserably weak. . . . The English are in a bad plight in the Transvaal. If the country would only have listened to us earlier, how many lives would have been saved."

Ouida to Wilfrid Scawen Blunt.

[1900.]

" It is frightful to think that the £114,000,000 wasted in this wicked war would have fed all these

poor famished natives and their animals.[1] How
dreadful, too, to deny them salt ! Here[2] the people
must not take a bucket of sea-water, lest they should
try to get a little salt by evaporating it in the sun.
Verily, in brutality of government, *tutto il mondo è
paese.*"

At the end of 1900 Ouida wrote some verses
embodying an appeal to Queen Victoria to stop the
war. She sent copies to those of her friends who
were, like herself, pronounced Pro-Boers. In forward-
ing them to Mr. Frederic Harrison she asked him
to get them published for her. The verses are of a
violent character, and entirely ignore the constitutional
position of a British sovereign. Mr. Harrison, very
naturally, refused to make any attempt in the direction
of publication, and Ouida was extremely indignant
with him, even accusing him of cowardice. In enclosing the verses to Mr. Blunt she wrote : " I send
you some verses which Frederic Harrison says would
cause any one who published them to pass two years
in prison. Yet I am sure Byron would have said
what I say in them, and history will do so " ; and to
Mr. Unwin under similar circumstances she said :
" I send you for your private pleasure and discretion
some verses which are I am sure what history will
say and Byron would have said."

[1] A reference to the famine in India.
[2] In Italy.

Ouida : a Memoir

A few lines, which may perhaps be quoted without offence, will serve to show something of the character of the poem, but it should be borne in mind that the verses breathe the vindictiveness that colours so much of Ouida's work and which is so often the result of lack of information about or insight into the real causes of things.

"Before your failing sight, the hot-red glare
Of burning homesteads must enflame the night.
Through your brief troubled sleep, the piteous cries
Of widowed women, homeless children, all
The human wreckage on the sea of war,
Must surely pierce your dull and weary ear!
The smoking cornfields, and the roofless hearths,
The tortured horses, and the hamstrung herds,
The whitening bones which choke the river's course,
The eyeless skulls which strew the flame-scorched plain,
Labour undone, youth slaughtered, childhood slain,
Mothers and virgins driven in flocks like sheep—
These visions, surely, in the dead of night,
Must make you weep that you have lived so long!

   .   .   .   .   .

Could you not, even in the chills of age,
Have found some strength to rise and to refuse?

   .   .   .   .   .

And to the Nation said, as your last word,
'I cannot lead: I will not follow you!
Death is too near: I dare not share a crime.
Leave my hands clean to fold on my dead breast."
Why did you not? So had your name been blest."

In a letter to Mr. Cockerell, to whom she also sent the " Victoria R. and I." verses, dated January 23,

1901, she had permitted herself a torrent of abuse of the Queen in prose which ended with the sentence:

"Worst of all, when her dogs were ill, or old, she sent them away and took new ones!"

And in a later letter to the same correspondent Ouida declared:—"The long reign of Victoria R. and I. has been a long triumph of the mediocrities, the hypocrisies, and the shams." She went on to say that she did not expect much of Edward VII, but "at least he is a man of the world, and he won't publish silly books in bad English."

Ouida had conceived a violent prejudice against royalty in general and contemporary sovereigns in particular. These views she embodied in her unfinished novel *Helianthus*, and also expressed them, often with an unmeasured violence of language which cannot be reproduced here, in letters to her friends.

Ouida to Sydney C. Cockerell.

"*April* 4, 1901.

"The late Queen[1] was always antagonistic to me. She had no real feeling for animals; in Landseer's pictures we see her with grallocked stags at her feet and her children playing with wild ducks just shot. . . .

"I enjoyed the article [2] of Mark Twain immensely,

---

[1] Victoria.

[2] Cf. *North American Review*, February, 1901, "To the Person sitting in Darkness," a very eloquent defence of the Chinese against the demands of the American Government for compensation in connection with the Boxer rising.

but usually he bores me with his ceaseless strain after jokes ; and he is very obtuse about many matters, being uneducated."

[*December* 8, 1901.]

" The state of the English mind is disgraceful. There is one thing the nation at least might do, *i.e.*, kick out the most brutal and inept of governments. What worse government can they possibly conceive? If I were a partizan of the war, I should despise it as much as I do being an opponent of the war. . . .

" Thanks for the Tolstoy. He is a great and eloquent writer,[1] but many of his opinions, such as those on the relations of the sexes, I think most mischievous. I cannot conceive how, with his genius, he can hold them.

" Have you read Wells's *Anticipations* ? They hold out a dreary and sickening prospect, and it makes one's heart ache to have had so little influence on the human mind, which has gone from bad to worse steadily throughout these twenty years, and grows only in one direction—that of scientific tyranny. . . .

" I have written next to nothing, but I have been four years, at wide intervals, creating a work of which more another day."

---

[1] In a later letter (December 23) Ouida says :—" Tolstoy is far from a great thinker—though a great writer."

Lucca

"The book [1] I named to you has been more than three years slowly creating itself. It is in a measure a satire on royalty. Would it be well or ill to issue it before the coronation? The English are rendering themselves odiously flunkey; and why choose mid-summer to sweat under ermine and velvet robes? Poor little ermines!—or are they kittens' tails?"

After reading Mr. A. M. S. Methuen's *Peace or War in South Africa* [2] Ouida wrote to the author :—

"I have read your book with sympathy and admiration. The style is lucid and eloquent : and the reasonings would convince any one whose mind was not closed by self-interest or stupidity.

"I cannot comprehend how even those who approve the war can approve the manner in which it is con-ducted and the disgraceful Ministry which boasts of death, disease, and defeat as of three gods in one."

Ouida to Sydney C. Cockerell.

"December 23 [1901].

"It is kind of you to send me *Erewhon*. I have never read it. There was far more wit thirty years ago, and more enjoyment of good literature. The tearing pace at which people live now is not conducive to intellectual brilliancy."

[1] *Helianthus.*   [2] Published 1901.

187

Ouida : a Memoir

The Tauchnitz edition of *Critical Studies* was published in 1901, but without the article on Chamberlain, and with the omission of certain passages reflecting on the German Emperor in the article on George Darien's novels. Ouida strongly objected to these omissions, over which there was much correspondence.

Ouida to Baron Tauchnitz.

[1901.]

"Do not send me any of the *Critical Studies*, as it would vex me to see the volume without its castigations of Joseph Chamberlain and your Kaiser."

Ouida's belief in her power to influence politics never left her, and in December, 1901, she wrote to Lord Rosebery, although she was not acquainted with him personally, in the hope that her words might bear fruit in a great speech he was to make at Chesterfield on the 19th of the month; she began by asking him how a man of his breeding could support Chamberlain, and was terribly disappointed when Lord Rosebery took no sort of notice of her appeal.

In 1902 Ouida had a project of going to England, which she had not visited since 1887. She wrote to Mr. Cockerell in March :—

"If I can afford it I shall come to England in the summer; there are many friends I want to see, and one loses much pecuniarily, never to see and speak with one's men of business."

188

Her native land was evidently much in her thoughts at this time, and she writes to him again in April :—

"The description of Essex makes me sigh for a little place my mother mortgaged and lost, she never knew very well how ; it was near Castle Hedingham and had oak-panelled rooms, and great elms in its meadows. I might have made an English pied à terre of it."

Public affairs and public men formed as usual the subjects of her letters, with an occasional expression of her disgust at the dog-laws of Italy.

Ouida to Sydney C. Cockerell.

"*April* 3 [1902].

"His [Cecil Rhodes] perspicacity was small ; *vide* his predictions at beginning of the war. I think he was kept dull and gross by his heavy eating and by the common men who were his associates. His love of classic literature would suggest that he had a soul in him somewhere. His death is pitiful. Africa makes Englishmen exceedingly coarse. It did not have that effect on Scipio and other Latins."

[*April* 27, 1902.]

"One hundred and fifty filthy Calabrians are sleeping on straw here in the beautiful cloister of S. Francesco, and they think a nice clean dog walking in the streets a peril to health ! ! !"

Ouida : a Memoir

"June 17, 1902.

"No, dear sir, I have no mixed feelings. I have an unmixed disgust and disappointment. I thought the Boers, at least, knew how to die, and would show the old Thermopylean spirit to the end. Whereas, everything collapses, and finishes in a grotesque and pantomime-like manner, and one does not see why or for what they have been resisting two years and eight months. . . . The whole thing is sickening and more like a Christmas burlesque than a chapter in the history of Great Britain."

Ouida's financial troubles now began to grow thick upon her. She had made no sort of provision for old age, or for the possibility of her vogue falling off, or for illness, all causes that might prevent her from writing. Her vanity did not allow her to take what she considered low fees for her stories, nor did it permit her to accept graciously the help that was readily forthcoming from her friends. Her glad acceptance or indignant refusal of such assistance depended, as we have seen, on her mood of the moment. Yet she never failed easily to reconcile herself to asking, and accepting, advances from her publishers for work to be done. And the readiness with which they responded to her appeals does honour to a profession that is sometimes not credited with the virtue of generosity.

In August, 1902, Ouida, in asking for further

advances for *Helianthus*,[1] told Baron Tauchnitz that she had " had nothing but losses all this year. When Fortune once frowns she remains sullen so long." The Baron acceded to her request and Ouida replied :

"DEAR FRIEND,—You are always kind. How beautiful a thing is kindness !—Would there were more of it in this life."

The Villa Massoni at Sant' Alessio, which Ouida had rented since 1894, belonged to Mme. Grosfils (*née* Massoni), wife of the Belgian Consul at Lucca. In the summer of 1903, wanting the villa, as she said, for her husband and family, she gave Ouida a short notice to quit. There are indications that things had not been going quite smoothly, for in a letter to Mr. Wilfrid Scawen Blunt dated April 20, Ouida wrote :—

" Can you tell me if there be revolvers small and light enough for me to fire, yet sternly effective ? My life is in danger here, and it is very necessary to be armed. Tell me what price one would be and the best maker."

Ouida asked for a little longer time, in view of the improvements she had made in the place, but her request was refused. Through Mr. Carmichael, the British Consul at Leghorn, Mme. Grosfils did all she could to induce Ouida to leave the villa in a quiet

---

[1] More than a year had passed since Ouida had promised him *Helianthus*. The novel was not published until after her death.

manner. One of the reasons given later by the Grosfils for their conduct was that they desired to protect Ouida from the threats of her creditors and their own property from eventual manumission. But Ouida was obdurate, and as peaceful measures availed nothing, Mme. Grosfils procured an eviction order for November 17th. Then she made a great mistake. Instead of waiting till that day, when in all probability Ouida would have left the house without giving trouble, on the afternoon of the 16th the sons of Mme. Grosfils took possession of the villa by force and treated Ouida in a disgraceful and cruel manner.

Ouida afterwards described what took place in letters to her friends. Writing to Sarmento in the following December, she complained in very strong language of the treatment she had received, and sent him a brief account of what took place. A year and a half later she wrote a detailed account to Baron Tauchnitz. It appears that on the afternoon in question the sons of Mme. Grosfils, accompanied by some rough men from their farms, broke into the grounds of the villa and proceeded to lock up two greenhouses containing some three hundred plants belonging to Ouida. They then entered the house. Ouida ordered them to go, but they insisted on remaining there, went into all the rooms, ransacked everything, locked up and affixed seals to each room, and flung all the MSS. and books they found into a box. Ultimately they kept by force all Ouida's paintings, china, books, unpublished MSS.

and letters from friends, especially the dispatch-box containing those written to her by Lord Lytton. When Ouida expostulated and protested they pursued her shrieking : " Si può rubare ! We shall seize everything ! everything is ours ! " They then went downstairs to a room next the kitchen, and sat there drinking, singing, and bawling till they fell asleep about 2 a.m. To continue in her own words :—

" At 7 a.m. they came up and insisted on me and my maid getting into a vehicle they had sent for and going to Viareggio (where I intended to go), eighteen miles, without bath or breakfast. I was foolish not to send for the carabiniers, but I was not sure what rights I had, as it was the last day, and I was very ill from fasting and sleeplessness. I took the dogs, of course ; they would not let me take anything else except some linen." [1]

After this " nuit d'enfer," as she characterized it, she reached the Hôtel de Russie, Viareggio, where she remained for the next seven months in a state of exhaustion bordering on prostration. She never really recovered from the shock she received that night.

It was not to be expected that Ouida would tamely submit to such treatment, and she proceeded at once to institute a case against the Grosfils in the ordinary court of Lucca.

[1] Letter to Baron Tauchnitz, June, 1905.

Ouida : a Memoir

Ouida to Sarmento.

[*December* 1, 1903.]

" I have left S. Alessio and have been vilely treated by the Grosfils, though I do not owe them a centime. What money and years wasted ! "

" *December* 18.

" I find this brouillon of what the Grosfils (did) and think you may like to read it.

" My lawyer here tells me it will be imprisonment and fines for them."

" *December* 22, 1903.

" The matter is in the hands of the law already. Thanks all the same.[1] The name is Grosfils. Her son broke open my box in her presence with a chisel ! The brouillon I sent you was for your own reading ; a more detailed copy had already gone to Rennell Rodd. I would not live at Viareggio if you gave me the town. Except the sea, it is everything I abhor. D'Annunzio's villino is a mere cotton-box with a dirty, dreary waste around it. The pines are nearly all cut down. The house has no view of the sea. By road it is four miles through an ugly flat country. He took it for six months and only stayed two. The contadino said that he '*piangeva tanto*.' I understand his tears in that howling desert ! From the back the place looks charming."

[1] For the address of a lawyer.

Lucca

The Grosfils and their relations left no stone un-turned in order to prevail on Ouida to condone the grave offence. This she absolutely refused to do, and so the legal proceedings slowly went their way. They included a criminal action for wrongful entry of her domicile and an action for damages with regard to the seizure of her property, the rent having been duly paid.

The literary output of this period included, besides the novel *The Massarenes* (1897) and the two volumes of collected essays, *Views and Opinions* (1895), and *Critical Studies* (1900), nothing of first-rate importance. Stories in the compass of one small volume and collections of short tales previously contributed to magazines were all that came from her pen. She turned them out with apparent ease, but seemed in-capable of any sustained effort in the way of writing. She never accomplished another long novel, and for the remaining years of her life her active brain found its chief outlet in letter-writing.

VI

LAST YEARS
AND DEATH
1904—1908

CHAPTER VI

LAST YEARS AND DEATH
1904–1908

IT is a remarkable fact that while Ouida was engaged in troublesome and disagreeable litigation with the Grosfils, she was able to detach her mind from the worries connected with it and to write the following interesting letters to Mr. Cockerell, interesting for the subject matter, and as a proof that she could now sometimes forget herself and contemplate literature and public affairs and the problems of life from an objective standpoint.

Mr. Cockerell had visited Tolstoy in 1903, and this led to a discussion of his qualities as a thinker and writer.

Ouida to Sydney C. Cockerell.

[VIAREGGIO],
" *January* 2 [1904].

" To me Tolstoy has not much intellect. Many of his doctrines are absolutely foolish. He has little judgment of literature, and not much, surely, of men.

199

His admiration of Dickens proves the non-intellectual fibre of his mind ; and his morality and monogamy are against common sense and nature.

.　　.　　.　　.　　.

"It is very injurious to my interests not to come to England, but (money apart) I have no one whom I can trust with the dogs. My maid likes them and has been with me twenty-three years, but I should not be sure of her if I were absent. You cannot trust Italians out of sight. The sea here is very beautiful and it has strengthened me ; but mentally I am wholly indisposed to do anything, even to read the papers ! What is the use of writing or speaking ? On ne prêche qu'aux convertis !—or rather it is only the ' déjà convertis ' who come to our church."

[VIAREGGIO, *January* 6, 1904.]

"Thanks for the Tolstoys. But I know all his views and arguments. When he says that ' any rational being requires to believe in a god,' he shows how limited his mind is. Probably if he had not been a Russian he would have been a much greater man. In many ways he is absolutely silly. In vulgar parlance, his doctrines ' will not wash.' Observe, too, how he ignores the fact that fighting is *natural* to man. See a little child's rage before it can speak ; its angry gestures, its inflamed face, its dumb fury. Men would not live in peace together if armies were abolished. Tolstoy does not realize that man is a very rudimentary, imperfect creature, occupying a very small place in an immense and unknown universe."

[VIAREGGIO, *January 23, 1904.*]

"Do not mistake me; I think Tolstoy a great novelist, a great character for courage and self-sacrifice; but I cannot think a man who believes in Christianity is a man of great intellect, and his logic is sadly defective in many other ways. He judges the rest of the world by Russia. . . .

"I mean to take the *Westminster Gazette*. It is the best of English papers, I think. . . .

"Surely the infants of to-day will be the men of twenty years hence; I do not believe the human race will ever be much altered; and it degenerates physically. War, as we know it, may end, because armies will mutually blow each other into space; but something equally bad will come in its stead, until the earth vanishes, as a scientist foresees, by the combustion of the atmosphere by electricity."

Ouida professed no dogmatic religion, a fact that had always troubled her relatives. Discussing the belief in the divinity of Christ with Mr. Cockerell, she asked what remained if that faith was no longer held, and herself replied to the question in words that serve to show her own point of view in these important matters.

"What of course was always there, a poor man of

fine instincts sore troubled by the suffering and the injustice which torment Tolstoy to-day. Christ drew the poor after him, naturally, by his assurances that the future would compensate them for their painful labour. But I have never been able to understand how theories so crude, so illogical, so uneducated and unsupported, could ever attract or satisfy intellectual minds. 'One must believe something' I am told. Why? Why should one need a belief? The whole of existence is a mystery; and science does not explain it more than ignorance. Tolstoy must know as well as I do that numbers of people are born hopelessly vile or bad; was Whittaker Wright tempted by poverty? The mere sentimental 'do unto others,' etc., etc., cannot restrain the passions, or rein in the appetites, or solve the problems of life. Tolstoy is dangerous because he is misleading. He is an educated Christ. If he had been born in France he would have been a great man, but the frightful life of Russia has disturbed his brain."

Ouida to Sydney C. Cockerell.

[VIAREGGIO, *February* 2, 1904.]

"What annoys me in Tolstoy is his 'cocksureness,' to use a vulgar but expressive term. He is so sadly far off from the wise 'Que scais-je?' of Montaigne. I should like to converse with him, but that will never be."

Last Years and Death

The progress of the Grosfils case may be learned best from Ouida's letters to Sarmento.

" Happily I do not want Conti ; [1] Aurelio [2] has bestirred himself and the *acte d'accusation* is gone to the Tribunal. I will send you a copy if you will please return it.

" F. M.[3] writes that he will do what I asked. He seems very pleasant.

" Thanks for name of British Ambassador.

" Do you know Bertie personally ?

" I can never understand how Crawford turns out books in the number he does. If he had written one-sixth the number he might have been a great novelist or at least a good one. But the public does not know mediocrity from excellence, or trumpery from beauty.

" PS.—Tell me all the people you see."

[*April* 15, 1904.]

" Thanks ; I have no idea where to go, but certainly je serai à votre portée. If possible I shall go to England, and I hope certainly to go to Brussels, as the Minister A.E. (affaires étrangères) there desires

---

[1] A lawyer whom Sarmento had recommended.
[2] Her own lawyer.
[3] Sir Frederick Macmillan.

to see me, and he will, I have no doubt, dismiss Grosfils. Their conduct has been too brutal and disgusts even their friends. It was only done in the hope of stealing the few objects I still possess. They have already stripped the place of timber and evergreens. It [1] is no longer worth anything. I intensely regret not having seen the Devonshires. I hope he will make a Ministry of his own. She is very nice to me and a woman of great talent.

"I wish you were here ; we could have long talks on the sands. I walk up to the Fosso del Abate, about three miles off ; that is my limit. Cannot you come now ? Rome must be very hot."

Now that the Boer War was a thing of the past, Ouida interested herself in the war between Russia and Japan, and her comments on it fill many pages of her letters at this period.

Ouida to Sydney C. Cockerell.

[*May* 24, 1904.]

"If Russia and Japan could eat up each other like the Kilkenny cats it would be well for the world. They are both cruel savages with a veneer of civilization. I remember my father saying when I was a child that the yellow races would overrun the European countries. Japan had unique, exquisite, and charming arts, costumes, and crafts of its own ; and

[1] Villa Massoni.

it can do nothing better than imitate like an ape the hideous and ludicrous modes of Europe and America with all their brutalities and vulgarities."

At the beginning of June Ouida left Viareggio for Bagni di Lucca and remained there for several months. She greatly disliked the place, and only chose it as a convenient residence during the litigation in which she was engaged. She found it damp, and the whole time she remained there suffered from cold and cough. Notwithstanding her many preoccupations, she found time and energy to carry on a large correspondence.

Ouida to Sydney C. Cockerell.

[BAGNI DI LUCCA, *June* 2, 1904.]

" DEAR ENTHUSIAST,—

"Let us await the end of the war; it is easier to begin a war than to limit it. Both these nations are hideously tyrannical and cruel, and these two crimes are surely the greatest of all on earth. 'On aime toujours contre q'q'un'; in this instance your Japanese love grows out of your Russian hate; I do not mean yours individually, but nationally."

[BAGNI DI LUCCA, *June* 5, 1904.]

" Intellectually the Japanese may be all you think, but the influence of their physique will be deplorable if the Europeans unite with them in physical union. . . .

Ouida : a Memoir

"Novels become so ridiculous in their numbers nowadays ; they disgust me with the art of fiction."

[BAGNI DI LUCCA, *June* 7, 1904.]

"I see nothing in that nation[1] to be desired as a future influence. Their stupid superstitions, their grovelling Emperor-worship, their rejection of love to the lowest place, their savage murders and suicides, seem to me to embody all which we most desire to eliminate from our own lives. Men who suffer so little physically as the yellow races must be cruel. They go to slaughter like a horde of ants ; and their war-craze is not heroism but a repetition of their suicidal mania. Patriotism is not what we want in Europe and America. It is a much wider, finer, more impersonal feeling. Some years ago men seemed to be approaching this ideal, but ever since the Franco-German War they have deteriorated in everything except mechanics ; and the bicycle and autocar are ruining them physically. You call this view pessimism ; it seems to me common sense."

[BAGNI DI LUCCA, *June* 26, 1904.]

"Europe and the U.S.A. are horribly vulgar in all their ways and thoughts and actions ; how much gentler, calmer, more graceful, and more courteous were the people of my childhood !"

[1] Japan.

Last Years and Death

" La Villa, Bagni di Lucca,
[*July* 7, 1904].

"I am this time wholly in accord with Tolstoy.[1]
But it is a pity he brings in Deity in various forms,
because the continuance of war through thousands
of years is inconsistent with the direction of a bene-
ficent and omnipotent God. I think, as I have always
done, that Tolstoy is a great genius but not a great
intellect. The two are distinct.

.   .   .   .   .

"It is so true that the intellect is powerless against
the passion for bloodshed."

[*July* 8, 1904.]

"What is the use of art or literature ? The world
is choked with over-production and the earth is
soaked with blood. I think it must have been better
in Etruscan times. They were so fond of their dogs !
So were the Romans. And they were honest about
their human slaves."

[Bagni di Lucca]
"*August* 25 [1904].

"It is this tendency,[2] so very retrograde and be-
littling, which I find so bad in the Japanese. Their
intelligence in a certain sense is, doubtless, great, but
in a moral sense it is snobbish and silly, and their
nature is cold and unlovely. If, as seems likely,

---

[1] See Tolstoy's statement on war in the *Times*, June 27, 1904.
[2] Belief in the monarchy.

they will come to dominate Europe, what have we gained, since we shall remain crawling before reigning Houses ?   Their physical influence will be certainly not desirable either."

" *December* 12 [1904].

"Your favourites [1] are winning all along the line. I do not know whether, eventually, it may be good for the human race. . . .

"Fisher Unwin sent me *The Vineyard* of Mrs. Craigie, so I read it.   I should imagine her comedies are better than her books, for her dialogues are good, but her action is trivial, and her force all goes away after the start.   Her descriptions of nature are poetic."

The case against the Grosfils was heard at the ordinary court of Lucca on December 19, 1904, and the verdict was in Ouida's favour, the two sons of Mme. Grosfils being sentenced to ten months' imprisonment and to pay all costs.

Ouida to Sarmento. [2]

" *December* 20, 1904.

" The two [3] decamped before the sentence was passed. If they had not they would have had a bad reception

[1] The Japanese.

[2] In a letter to him dated December 4th, she wrote : " It is very melancholy here [Bagni di Lucca], and all that is worth anything in life has gone away from me, and it is not likely I shall ever recover it."

[3] The two sons of Mme. Grosfils.

GEO. SARMENTO
Bagni di Lucca
sep. 1904

[*Photo by Emery Walker.*

OUIDA IN 1904.

From a chalk drawing by Sarmento in the National Portrait Gallery, London.

To face p. 208.

from the public. The judge treated them with contumely. 'Stand down,' he said to Henri G. ; 'every word you utter is a lie. Che vergogna! (Shame upon you!)'

"The Procuratore del Re asked for a year's imprisonment. Certainly they will go to prison ; all the Appello (Court of Appeal) is likely to do is to cut off a month or so ; but the sentence is not as long as it should be, even now.

"They are shut up at the villa with the rest of the family, except their parents, who are believed to have gone to Brussels. I telegraphed the sentence to the Belgian Foreign Minister, and wrote to him ; I conclude he will oblige the Grosfils to resign the Consulate.

"The people of Lucca are delighted.

"They say I spoke very well ; and I curtseyed to the judge, which nobody else did. Gori (my maid) gave her evidence splendidly ; so clearly and lucidly, it was really she who smashed them. Two of their witnesses gave false evidence and the judge detected it."[1]

---

[1] The widow of an English diplomatist who was present at the trial sent Sarmento the following details : "Ouida looked *quite regal* in a *long* black dress and ditto cloak, lined with grey plush, and a black hat with ostrich plumes. The only tiresome thing about her was that she would keep on interrupting when evidence was given against her, in a shrill, high voice: 'Ma chè ! ma chè ! ha ! ha ! ha ! chè buggia (What a lie !),' etc., etc. Counsel

O

Ouida : a Memoir

The Grosfils, however, determined to appeal against the sentence, and took the case up to the Court of Appeal at Lucca, which, however, saw no reason to reverse the decision of the ordinary court. But they were not yet satisfied, and took it still further, to the Court of Cassation at Rome. Meantime, of course, no costs or damages were paid by the culprits, and Ouida was in the usual straits for money. She assured Tauchnitz in April, 1905: "The costs in this process will all be ultimately paid back to me with damages, but meantime they leave me penniless."

Now before March, 1903, Ouida had signed an agreement with Messrs. Macmillan on generous terms for her novel of *Helianthus*. By April, 1905, she had sent them only a few chapters of the manuscript, and those in a very confused state, but had received from them a large sum of money, representing, indeed, the greater part of the amount agreed on for advance royalties. The firm, however, continued to advance her money, and even at her request to pay small bills for her and do commissions for her. She told Mr. Carmichael that the Macmillans behaved "like angels" to her over the book, which was issued incomplete after her death.

She was living now under most wretched conditions.

appealed to one who was sitting behind Ouida, pathetically, saying in Italian: '*Please do all you can to keep her quiet*, as if she goes on like that it will be bad for the case.'"

Last Years and Death

Ouida to Sydney C. Cockerell.

[VIAREGGIO]
"*February* 10 [1905].

" The cold of this winter has entered into me, and I cannot get rid of its results. I am unwell ; and *Helianthus* lies disregarded. The frightful state of Russia is sickening. The Tsar and his five uncles should all be sent to Siberia."

Ouida to Baron Tauchnitz.

[*May* or *June*, 1905.]

" Unfortunately there is a third court, called Cassazione, designed in the rare event of any justice being done to undo it. They are going to appeal there. It is in Rome."

" PONTE SERRAGLIO,
" BAGNI DI LUCCA,
" *June* 27 [1905].

" You will be glad to hear that my enemies having carried the case to the Court of Cassation in Rome, that Court promptly decided against them. There is now no Court left to which they can appeal, so to prison they go. My lawyers will now levy the costs and indemnity on their property. The case has lasted nineteen months ! They were utter idiots to attempt any defence. . . .

" It is very beautiful here, on the river Lima, which Shelley loved."

Ouida : a Memoir

"August 4 [1905].

" You were quite right that it was a terrible risk to run, to embark on this litigation ; but I had no choice. I was forced either to prosecute or meekly to have my throat cut. As yet I have not been reimbursed a farthing, although they are legally condemned to pay all costs and damages."

By a Royal act of clemency which roused all Ouida's fury, the sentence was commuted to a fine and the culprits allowed to leave the country. The civil action for damages and recovery of her property was going on during the rest of Ouida's life, and is still unheard ; the matter is now in the hands of the curator of her estate.

Ouida never recovered the personal effects that had been carried off by the Grosfils ; they declared they kept the property to indemnify themselves for the damage Ouida had done to the house, in spite of her declaration that she had spent large sums of money in improving the place.

But her sense of her own importance remained as strong as ever. It was about this time that Mrs. Conway Thornton first saw Ouida, and on her return to her hotel after the meeting received the following note :—

" DEAR MRS. THORNTON,—As you were so kind as not to ask for an autograph, I send you mine.—OUIDA."

Last Years and Death

Ouida now made a new friend, by correspondence, so to speak, for she never met him in the flesh. For years she had taken great interest in the family who owned Hardwick House, Bury St. Edmunds, in the grounds of which she had been accustomed to walk as a girl. She expressed a wish to mutual friends to know Mr. G. Milner-Gibson-Cullum,[1] the present owner, who succeeded to the estate of Hardwick in 1878, and wrote to him, proposing an interview, which, however, never took place. But a pleasant intimate correspondence was instituted that lasted till a month before her death. When Mr. Cullum could have gone to visit her, she was too ill to see any one. In telling him that she had won her case against the Grosfils she wrote : " But in law, as in war, the next costliest thing to defeat is victory."

Ouida to G. Milner-Gibson-Cullum.

[Bagni di Lucca]
"*March* 29 [1905].

" Thanks for all you so kindly say of me. It would be better for me if I had never seen Italy. I wish, indeed, that I had known your gifted mother ;[2]

---

[1] Son of the Right Hon. Thomas Milner-Gibson, M.P., and his wife Susanna Arethusa, only child of Sir Thomas Gery Cullum, Bart. He added his maternal family name to the others in 1878.

[2] Mrs. Milner-Gibson was the friend of Dickens and Thackeray, and her salon in London was famous from 1840 to 1870, and afterwards in Paris till her death in 1885. She opened her doors

but she never approached me, though we were near many times. If I had Hardwick I would live in a corner of it and never leave it. You moderns waste all your time and your substance in movement."

In November, 1905, Ouida left Bagni di Lucca for Viareggio.

Ouida to G. Milner-Gibson-Cullum.

" I shall not be in the Bagni di Lucca ever again, for I hate the place. The sun rises at 10, and goes over the hills at 4, in summer ! They have beautiful trees, but they are always chopping and lopping them for firewood. I stayed there to be near Lucca for a lawsuit which I won in Lucca, and finally in Rome, Court of Cassazione. ' Spese ' and ' danni ' were ordered to be paid to me, but it is not likely that I shall ever see a farthing of them."

She occupied herself in reading, in writing quantities of letters, and in looking after her numerous dogs.

Ouida to Sydney C. Cockerell.

[VIAREGGIO]
" *August* 31 [1905].

" I saw the eclipse magnificently yesterday ; some dun and gold clouds overhung a great wooded hill

to all exiled patriots. She had a genuine instinct of hospitality, and made it her aim to give pleasure to others and to see those around her happy. Cf. Edmund Yates, *Recollections*, i. 252–3.

and in a clear space in their centre hung the sun, four-fifths black with shadow. It was a beautiful and mysterious sight. Very few people saw it.

" Of all the imbecile and wicked manias the craze of sport seems to be the most odious. The Marquis Simari, a famous sportsman, is just dead ; he shot for a wager 1,000 swallows and killed every one ! "

" December 31 [1905].

" It is a strong Ministry, with its weak point at its apex. I do not envy John Burns his task of reconciling the irreconcilable. Do you think it will last, and win the elections? I confess I cannot understand the policy of Chamberlain. He seems to me to have given himself away in the most idiotic manner. The alliance between him and the Tories was always unholy and grotesque. I hope my friend Curzon will ' sit tight ' and spare not. If his health spares him he will have a great future."

[Viareggio, January 11, 1906.]

" I wish you would remind people that twenty years ago, when society was beginning to adore Joe[1] and see in him the Messiah, I was six months in London, and I told several of the leaders, male and female, of the Tory party what a curse and ruin he would prove to them. They jeered at me and persisted in

---

[1] I.e., Chamberlain.

seeing in the greatest foe they possessed an angelic messenger. It was incomprehensible to me, and is so still. The D. of Devonshire was not a bit wiser than the others."

Ouida to G. *Milner-Gibson-Cullum.*

[Viareggio,]
" *May* 8 [1906 ?].

" If we live, we certainly shall meet before long, as if I do not go to Ardenza (Leghorn) I shall go to a villa a few miles from here, where you can easily come for a day,[1] and see d' Annunzio as well. I am not well, and cough enough to carry a strong man to his tomb. I hope, however, it will not take me to mine, for the dogs' sake. How you must long for the Hardwick hawthorns ! "

Ouida to Sarmento.

"Viareggio,
"*November* 5, 1906.

" As regards my not writing books, I do not care for it. I do not feel any inclination or what people call inspiration. I have never written except when the spirit moves [me]. I see that the state of the world is infinitely worse than twenty years ago and one cannot alter its tendencies."

[1] Cullum was staying at Salsomaggiore.

Last Years and Death

Ouida to Sydney C. Cockerell.

[*November* 8, 1906.]

"I am much distressed to see this a.m. the death of Auberon Herbert.[1] He was a great friend and constant correspondent of mine for many years. It was a pity his eccentricities obscured the real brilliancy and admirable intuitions of his mind. Most people saw the absurdities of the surface, and did not see the mine of wisdom beneath."

[*February* 16, 1907.]

"I should have liked to see Asquith when in Rome, but could not afford to go there. Americans make the prices exorbitant. I wish the great city had a better use than being a hostelry for Yankees."

Ouida to Sarmento.

" *February* 18, 1907.

"I am glad you have a fine view ; it is a great consolation.

"I have been very ill and miserable ; now I am somewhat better and stronger. The weather is superb, but I am not able to walk much . . .

---

[1] Cf. the article on Auberon Herbert in *Critical Studies* (1900), where she says : "Auberon Herbert is known to the world as a daring and original thinker, a sociologist who lives three centuries before his time, a fearless preacher of new liberties and ideal creeds."

Ouida : a Memoir

" I told you of my dear, dear Lello's[1] death ; he is an unutterable loss to me ; and for thirty hours he suffered very greatly. . . .

" If I had not the dogs I think I would go and end my days in England.   Italy has been a great ingrate to me."

Ouida to G. Milner-Gibson-Cullum.

[VIAREGGIO, *April*, 1907.]

" I have never muzzled a dog in my life.   Here it is the law for July and August, so for those months I must be elsewhere ; besides, it is too hot here for me after May 15th.   Yes, the demolition of beautiful old buildings is an agony to all those who have eyes to see and souls to feel ; but these are few in the actual days."

Ouida to Sydney C. Cockerell.

" *May* 13 [1907].

" People change as life goes on ; *I* do not.   I think I am exactly what I was when very young, in opinions and character."

In 1907 there was a grand historical pageant in the Abbey Gardens at Bury St. Edmunds, and Mr. Cullum seems to have suggested that Ouida should come over for it.   In her letters to him occur passages

---

[1] One of her favourite dogs.

218

that show, ill and lonely and poor as she now was, she still retained her inordinate vanity.

Ouida to G. Milner-Gibson-Cullum.

[1907.]

" What a curse it is to have anything which distinguishes one from the happy unknown multitude!

" If I came to Bury I should come incognita as Contessa di Sant' Alessio ; poor Mr. Oakes offered me all sorts of honours, but I told him nothing could be more odious to me."

And again—

[VIAREGGIO, *April,* 1907.]

" It would divert me greatly to come in July and be presented by you as a Florentine or Roman lady who was very kind to you when you were ill with enteric fever !—then we would talk of Ouida and abuse her."

" VIAREGGIO,

" *May* 24 [1907].

" Pray remember to keep me au courant with the incidents of the festival. Keep my name out of it as much as you can."

In April, 1907, Ouida was approached through Mr. Carmichael, the British Consul at Leghorn, by an English publisher with regard to bringing out her autobiography or memoirs. Ouida declared that she never intended to write any memoirs.

Ouida : a Memoir

Ouida to Montgomery Carmichael.

" *May* 2 [1907].

" I think memoirs, even those delicious memoirs of France, are base betrayals of others, and show great vanity in the writers. To possess any interest they must be treacheries—in general to the dead, who cannot defend themselves. The inquisitive temper which makes such revelations sought by the public is surely an appetite to be discouraged."

Ouida desired it to be made clear to all whom it concerned that in her view memoirs could " only be made agreeable to the public by base treasons to others, and want of dignity in oneself." [1] She referred to the subject again in August :—

" Please don't ever speak of an autobiography, or we shall quarrel. I despise and hate all such things ; what vanity must beget it ! " [2]

That her feeling in the matter was sincere there can be no manner of doubt, for the publisher in question was willing to pay Ouida well for such a volume, and she was suffering at this time from want of money. The Grosfils had paid her nothing. She was spending the summer months in small lodgings at Mazzarosa, a little place near Viareggio, where she was " perfectly wretched." She feared

---

[1] Letter to Montgomery Carmichael, May 9, 1907.
[2] *Ibid.*, August 1, 1907.

Last Years and Death

if she left Tuscany altogether the Grosfils would triumph, and as she put the comfort of her dogs before her own, and the muzzling order prevailed, she found it difficult to remain there. Indeed, she wrote to Mr. Carmichael, " I know not where to go to live." [1]

In July, 1907, a report was spread by the English Press that Ouida was in want and great distress. Although there was much truth in the statement, it was some exaggeration of the actual state of affairs. In any case, it seems to have been almost impossible to help Ouida, for she had no idea how to economize or how to regulate the expenditure of a small income, and to the very last preferred to feed her own and any stray dogs rather than to feed herself. One of her friends who read this report sent her a cheque, which she accepted after some demur in a letter dated July 21, saying, " Matters are not so bad as they are represented. I have been seven months at the Hôtel Grand Bretagne, so could not have died of hunger."

A sister novelist wrote a sympathetic letter to the editor of the *Daily Mail*, suggesting that a fund should be started to relieve Ouida's distress, and enclosing a cheque for £25 as a first contribution. Ouida was terribly angry when she read this, and sent the editor a telegram absolutely forbidding him to make any mention of her in his

[1] May, 1907.

paper. Others tried to help her, but their efforts were equally in vain. Vernon Lee, for instance, saw the published accounts of Ouida's distress. She asked a friend, an English trained nurse who was just then at Bagni di Lucca, to go to Mazzarosa, and find out what could be done for her, and to do it. The lady found the little house in which Ouida was lodging and was told that she did not wish to receive anybody. She had been ill, but was now recovering, was up, and able to spend some time each day in the garden with her dogs. She had really been turned out of the hotel on account of her dogs and of unpaid bills, and had taken refuge in the house of some humble people who knew her. The landlady said that many visitors called, but that Ouida would see none of them except the secretary of the Prefect of Lucca and Mr. Carmichael.

Ouida to Montgomery Carmichael.

[*July*, 1907].

" I receive scores of letters, ' anguish,' ' unspeakable sympathy,' etc. Of course my *intimate* friends have not believed it. What am I to do to wash this mud off my name ? "

Ouida consulted with her friends as to whether she could take action against the paper that had published these exaggerated reports of her condition.

Last Years and Death

Ouida to Montgomery Carmichael.

[*July,* 1907.]

" Meanwhile it is enormously painful and injurious to me. For the saying of Voltaire is so true : ' Calumniez, calumniez, calumniez ! toujours quelque-chose restera.' There will always be many who will believe I was starving on the seashore, though I was seven months at the Hotel Gran Bretagna and left there ten days ago ; they are not people to have let me depart had I not paid them the uttermost farthing. . . .

" I do not know where to go. I should like to go out of Italy forever and forever."

Some of Ouida's influential friends, recognizing the difficulty of relieving her distress privately, had, however, before this suggested a public subscription. When the plan came to Ouida's ears she was most indignant, and declared that she wanted for nothing. Then they approached the Prime Minister, Mr. Campbell-Bannerman, and succeeded in procuring for her a Civil List pension of £150 a year for life. This, too, she declined, remarking to a friend, " What right have they to offer me a pension only fit for superannuated butlers?" [1] Ultimately she was prevailed on to accept it, and she did so in a letter dated July

[1] There seems to have been some misapprehension at first in regard to the amount.

16, 1906. It was granted to her in the August of that year, to date from April 1, 1906. It seems that Ouida was very touchy about the publicity and what she considered the humiliation of a pension, and so the co-operation of her old friend, Winifred, Lady Howard of Glossop, who by 1906 had rather drifted apart from her, but who knew Ouida's moods, was invited, and it was chiefly due to her that Ouida's scruples were finally overcome. But, unhappily, when the cheques came in, they went immediately to pay pressing creditors.

Towards the close of 1906 Ouida had lost the sight of the right eye. Writing to Mr. Cockerell in February, 1907, she told him, "It is no disfigurement, but the sight is gone. And my sight has been so wonderful. Last autumn I could see the satellites of Jove without a glass." In mentioning the matter to Tauchnitz in April she wrote :—

" It is a great sorrow, as my eyes have been a source of infinite joy to me and were as clear and strong of vision as in youth !

" *Helianthus* stands unfinished still, and the kindness of the Macmillans has been most constant and beyond all praise."

The injury to the eye was really the result of exposure, and the following letter tells the cause and manner.

Last Years and Death

"It would take folios to tell you all that has befallen me ; nearly all painful.   I left Camaiore in September, in haste, on account of the muzzling order and drove with the four dogs one evening into Viareggio, never doubting to be received at the (hotel) Russie.

"Instead, it and all V. were overcrowded.   I could not get a room anywhere nor even a sitting-room to stay in for the night.   It grew late ; I was obliged to hire the fiacre for the night, and the man took out his horse and went away ; I was left with my dogs in the Station Piazza ; happily it was a full moon, for the cab lamp went out in an hour.   I had no extra covering, and it was very damp.

"The next day my eye was very inflamed, and it became the affection known as glaucoma.   In a month I was blind in that eye.   In the external appearance of the eye there is no change, but the blindness is incurable.   It is not at all a rare thing, though I never heard of it, did you ?

"I think it was odious of S., where I and the dogs had been seven winter months, as you will remember, not to take me at least under his roof.[1]   It was very dangerous for a lady to be absolutely alone throughout a long night, and I had a black valise which looked valuable.   I had sent my maid to sleep at her mother's

[1] Hotel de Russie.

225   P

early in the afternoon and I forgot her address. In the morning she found me. It was very disagreeable. The Viareggini are great brutes.

"I mourn infinitely the loss of my right eye. One can never tell that the other may not be affected by sympathy. How could I bear my life if I were sightless?

"My sight has always been so strong and clear, and as far-reaching as when I was ten years old.

"Alas! The left eye is, as I say, all right, but how long may it be so? There is great sympathy between the eyes.

"No one cares. It does not matter to anybody."

About this time Ouida wrote to Sir Rennell Rodd that the end of her life "was destined to be like that of an old horse, all misery."

Her troubles with the journalists were not yet at an end. The *Daily Mirror* published what purported to be a portrait of Ouida : it was really that of an old peasant woman sitting in a field, reading. Her vanity was hurt beyond repair.

Ouida to T. Fisher Unwin.

[MAZZAROSA]
" *August* 1, 1907.

"You do not mention the singular libel and calumny of the *Daily Mail* and other papers upon me. It is all a lie, and a very strange one. A young corre-

Last Years and Death

spondent of the *D. M.* called and wanted to see me ; I did not receive him ; this was his vengeance. The 'portrait' so called by the *Daily Mirror* is an invention."

Ouida to G. Milner-Gibson-Cullum.

[*August*, 1907.]

" You will have seen the villainy of the *Daily Mail* and *Daily Mirror*. I believe it will cost them dear."

[*September*, 1907.]

" I cannot tell you the fury those vile issues of the *D. M.* excited in me ; and that abominable portrait of the old woman has gone all over the world as myself ! "

Ouida wrote to Mr. Carmichael that she thought an imaginary portrait the worst libel of all. " Could they not let me die in peace ? "

There is little more to record. Ouida's health became worse and worse, and she grew more and more eccentric and unreasonable. She spent most of her money on her dogs, and would even bring into the house mongrels from the street.

Ouida to Sydney C. Cockerell.

" Mazzarosa presso Viareggio,

" *August* 28 [1907].

" I have been very unwell ever since I wrote[1] with a dreadful cough and a sense of utter exhaustion and

[1] July 30.

227

weariness, physical and mental. The heat has been great even here, which is densely wooded and so has deep shadow. I have suffered much in many ways, but I hope the worst is past."

She returned to Viareggio in September. An attack of influenza was followed by inflammation of the lungs, and from this illness she never rallied.

Ouida to Sydney C. Cockerell.

[VIAREGGIO]
"*November* 8 [1907].

" You have not heard from me on account of a long illness from inflammation of the lungs which has kept me prostrate here (Viareggio) since the middle of September. I am convalescent, but still confined to my chamber."

On the 26th, in a pathetic letter to Mrs. Huntington,[1] she asks her not to tell people she found her looking ill,[2] says she has had fourteen years of almost continual trouble, and that perhaps she had made a mistake in going to Sant' Alessio, as it isolated her from society.

She continued to write letters to friends till a week before her death.

[1] Printed in H. C. Huntington's *Places, Memories*, 1911.
[2] "I hear you would not have known me, I am so changed."

OUIDA'S TOMB AT BAGNI DI LUCCA.

By Giuseppe Norfini,

To face p. 256.

Last Years and Death

Ouida to Sydney C. Cockerell.

"*Wednesday, January* 8 [1908].

"It is horrible weather here, raining and blowing and very cold. I cannot leave my room and I do not think I shall live long. . . . Do not say this about me, please."

[*January* 17, 1908.]

"I have been very ill all these days, and my maid is of opinion that I shall never get well. The weather is intensely cold; and at St. Remo it is so so warm and brilliant; it is odd there should be so great a difference. Excuse this rough word; I am ill and cannot write well.

"Ever yours,

"O."

Her greatest grief at the idea of death was that she must leave her "dear dogs." "Their lives," she wrote to Sir Squire Bancroft, "are too short in comparison with their devotion."

Ouida died of the effects of pneumonia at 70, Via Zanardelli, Viareggio, early on the morning of Saturday, January 25, 1908.

She had always used quill pens, and on a writing-table at the foot of the bed where her dead body lay were found, reverently arranged by her servant, two large quills in saltire.

Ouida was buried in the English cemetery at Bagni di Lucca. A lady who desires to remain anonymous—

her name, indeed, is only known to Mr. Carmichael—
paid the whole expense of a monument over her
grave. It represents the recumbent figure of Ouida
with a dog at her feet, the idea being taken from
Jacopo della Quercia's tomb of Ilaria del Cazetto in
the Duomo at Lucca, and is a dignified piece of
work by Giuseppe Norfini, who is also the sculptor
of the bust that forms the frontispiece of this volume.
Exaggeration pursued Ouida to the end, for the inscription commemorates her as "writer of incomparable
novels."

The *Daily Mirror* made amends for its errors by
starting the *Daily Mirror* Ouida Memorial Fund, to
assist which a matinée was given at the Lyceum
Theatre on March 10, 1908, when a dramatized
version of *Under Two Flags* formed the chief item
in the programme. Mr. Milner-Gibson-Cullum
worked very hard for the fund, both among Ouida's
friends in general and in her birthplace, Bury St.
Edmunds, where a memorial drinking fountain for
horses and dogs was erected in 1909. It was designed
by the sculptor Ernest J. Gillick, and is decorated with
a medallion portrait of Ouida and two allegorical figures
representing Justice and Sympathy. The inscription,
composed by Earl Curzon of Kedleston, runs :—

"Born at Bury St. Edmunds January 1st, 1839. Died at Viareggio,
Italy, January 25th, 1908. Her friends have erected this fountain
in the place of her birth. Here may God's creatures whom she
loved assuage her tender soul as they drink."

THE OUIDA MEMORIAL AT BURY ST. EDMUNDS.

By Ernest J. Gillick,

To face p. 230.

Last Years and Death

Ouida reveals her character so clearly in the letters contained in the foregoing pages that any special summation of it seems superfluous. Many will endorse Mr. Henry James's verdict, expressed to the writer of this memoir : "She was *curious*, in a common, little way . . . of a most uppish or dauntless little spirit of arrogance and independence . . . a little terrible and finally pathetic *grotesque*." But even he, as we shall see later, admired her perception of the beauty of Italy. Students of psychology, and those who have sympathy with human weakness and human failings, will recognize the pathetic side of such self-revelation as is to be found in this record of Ouida's career.

She saw everything through the magnifying glass of her own vanity. She exaggerated everything, both within and without herself : her talents, her own feelings and actions, and the actions and feelings of others towards herself. In judging Ouida, despite even the sadness of her last days, I scarcely think we should pity her overmuch, or conclude that because her life seems unhappy to the onlooker it was necessarily unhappy to herself. Inordinately vain persons are seldom unhappy ; they suffice unto themselves. As George Eliot put it, "they carry their comfort about with them." They are wholly wrapped up in their own affairs, and their illusion as to their own importance and influence hides from them, as by a thick curtain, the estimation in which they are held by others. Such self-absorption characterized Ouida

231

Ouida : a Memoir

from childhood : the habit grew on her until it became ingrained, and she came to regard herself rather as a heroine of one of her own books than as an ordinary woman living in an ordinary world.

It is, however, quite certain that Ouida possessed considerable powers of attraction. She numbered among her friends and acquaintances throughout her life some of the most interesting and famous men of the time. When some who knew her declare that she had no conversational talent, that she kept all her cleverness for her books, it may be that she did not always think it worth while to put forth her powers. Men will go to see a woman who is reputed to be clever or eccentric, or in some way distinguished from the multitude, once, or even twice, but they will not go often, or carry on with her a frequent correspondence extending over years, unless they derive from such intercourse pleasure and satisfaction. The few women, too, to whom she extended her friendship had affection for her and were staunch to the end. And it should never be forgotten that her friends from her earliest youth were in the habit of constantly stimulating her vanity.

In many ways, indeed, Ouida was no one's enemy but her own. Her curious lack of conscience about money was perhaps rather non-moral than immoral, and such an attitude with persons of Ouida's temperament is more common than is generally supposed. It is less easy to find excuse for the spirit of

revenge that made her pillory in *Friendship*
those who were, so she chose to imagine, instrumental
in preventing her marriage with Stufa. Looked at
dispassionately, such a spirit merely proves her
incapable of the love that gives all and demands
nothing, the kind of love she is always preaching to
the injured wife in *Guilderoy*, and the kind of love,
strangely enough, with which she endowed her many
heroines who are deserted by their lovers. The bitterness that enters her novels after the end of the seventies
is due to the same revengeful spirit, which is one of
Ouida's ugliest qualities, and led her only too often
to misjudge the characters of the persons, and
especially of the women, with whom she came in
contact.

We either smile at or deplore the extravagant
affection Ouida lavished on dumb animals, but beneath
the exaggeration we should perhaps see the very human
need, stronger in women than in men, for something
to love and take care of. Dumb animals are less
exacting than human beings, less likely to be faithless,
and to a woman of Ouida's temperament probably
more satisfactory objects of love. For it cannot be
denied that in her intercourse with human beings
Ouida gave little and demanded much in return.

Leaving aside the exaggeration, it must be admitted
that Ouida was not alone in her love of animals.
Both Mary Russell Mitford and Elizabeth Barrett
Browning in their letters express their affection for

their dogs in what to some might seem extravagant terms. When Flush, the dog that Miss Mitford had given Miss Barrett, was lost, its owner declared that she could "neither sleep, nor eat, nor do anything more rational than cry." Miss Mitford, in deploring the death of a favourite dog, wrote : "He loved me so entirely, and I, as entirely as is compatible with our far more selfish human nature, loved him," and went on to praise "his sweetness, his gentleness, his affection, his over-estimate of kindness, his forgetfulness of wrong, his recollection of old friends." But neither Miss Mitford nor Mrs. Browning committed the extravagance of treating dumb animals as if they were on a level with or above human beings.

Ouida said of Cecil Rhodes that he had a soul somewhere, and so it was with Ouida herself. She sympathized deeply with all who were suffering or oppressed ; she loved beauty in every form. In the letter from Mr. Henry James already referred to, he writes : "The best and most sincere thing about her I seemed to make out was—or had been—her original genuine perception of the beauty, the distinction and quality of Italy : this almost inspired her." She was generous to those in need, as many a poor Italian peasant could have testified ; she showed much kindness to, and took much interest in, young writers. She had high ideals which made her discontented with everyday life, but she blundered after

DETAIL OF THE FIGURE OF OUIDA ON HER TOMB AT BAGNI DI LUCCA.]

To face p. 234.

them in a semi-passionate and clumsy fashion, and never understood that—

> "The common problem, yours, mine, every one's,
> Is—not to fancy what were fair in life,
> Provided it could be—but, finding first
> What may be, then find how to make it fair
> Up to our means."

Let us then remember that her vehement expressions and unconsidered acts were blind strivings after the amelioration of the lot of the suffering and oppressed.

Notwithstanding the high estimate she held of her position as a writer, she had a strong objection to certain sorts of publicity. She was never interviewed by the Press. She disliked to be, as she phrased it, "made a show of," yet, as has been stated, she equally disliked to be caught by visitors "en déshabille." She objected to the publication of letters, and in fear of this enjoined on many of her friends the destruction of those she had written to them. She considered that the public had no possible title to enter into the pale of an artist's private life. But she summed up this feeling in words which show that modesty was scarcely its motive power :—

"The great man and the great woman should say to the world : 'Think of me what you choose. It is indifferent to me. You are not my master ; and I shall never accept you as a judge.' This should be the attitude of all royalty, whether that of King, the hero, or the genius." [1]

[1] Cf. "Vulgarity," in *Views and Opinions* (1895).

VII

OUIDA AS
NOVELIST

CHAPTER VII

OUIDA AS NOVELIST

IN a letter to *The Times*,[1] reprinted in *Frescoes*,
entitled " Romance and Realism," Ouida makes
what may be regarded as an apologia for her
particular form of fiction. She says : " I have,
I believe, been accused of writing ' fairy-stories ' ;
but is not life itself very often a fairy-story,
if too often, alas ! one in which the evil genius
preponderates and the wishing-cap is foolishly used
by the unwise ? . . . To many of us—to myself, I
confess, among the number—the world seems a marvellous union of tragedy and comedy, which run side
by side like twin children : like a ' web of Tyrian
looms ' with the gold threads crossing and recrossing
on the dusky purple of its intricate meshes. . . . I do
not object to realism in fiction ; what I object to
is the limitation of realism in fiction to what is
commonplace, tedious, and bald—is the habit, in a
word, of insisting that the potato is real and that the
passion-flower is not. . . . I cannot suppose that my

[1] October 12, 1883.

239

own experiences can be wholly exceptional ones, yet I have known very handsome people, I have known very fine characters, I have also known some very wicked ones, and I have also known many circumstances so romantic that were they described in fiction they would be ridiculed as exaggerated and impossible.

"A lecturer in the North of England, lecturing on my novels, remarked with *naïveté* and incredulity on the number of residences assigned in *Moths* to Prince Zouroff. Now, had the lecturer taken the trouble to inquire of any one conversant with the world, he would have learned that most great persons of all nationalities have three or four different residences at the least, and that a Russian noble is invariably extravagant in these matters. . . . Would it not be well if lecturers or reviewers, before calling everything which seems strange to themselves unreal or unnatural, were visited with a wholesome doubt as to whether it might not be their own experiences which were limited ? "

No one would be inclined to dispute the fact that Ouida sedulously avoided the cultivation of the potato and devoted herself exclusively to that of the passion-flower. It is only the greatest artists in fiction who see life steadily and see it whole. When we leave the heights, we must perforce be content with a more circumscribed view of things. A great novelist, too, may take a circumscribed area for his field of action ; Jane Austen succeeded perfectly in the very restricted limits of life that came within her ken, partly because she possessed the gift of humour, in which Ouida was wholly deficient, and partly because her insight enabled her to see human beings as they really were, are, and ever will be. It never seems to have occurred to Ouida that it takes all sorts of people to make up the world, and that the lives of all sorts and conditions of men and women afford material for the artist whose command of his art enables him so to present them that they are convincing and interesting to the reader. Some marriages are happy, others are not. Some women console themselves with a lover when the husband is not satisfactory, others do not. Some men are faithless to their wives, others are faithful to them. Some people are extravagant and self-indulgent, others are thrifty and self-denying, and so the world wags. Ouida never saw human beings of any kind as they really are, but always as she imagined them to be. Most of her men and women, regarded as such, too much resemble the childish daubs that form the paintings on which she so vastly prided herself. Some of her Italian and French peasants, however, are exceptions.

Nevertheless, she had her own high conception of the true artist, and often gives expression to it. In an essay entitled "The Penalties of a Well-known Name"[1] she writes :—

" The supreme gift of the true artist is a rapidity of perception and comprehension which is totally unlike

---

[1] Cf. *Views and Opinions* (1895).

the slow piecemeal observations of others. As the musician reads the page of a score at a glance, as the author comprehends the essence of a book by a flash of intelligence, as the painter sees at a glance the points and lines and hues of a landscape, whilst the ordinary man plods through the musical composition note by note, the book page by page, the landscape detail by detail, so the true artist, whether poet, painter, or dramatist, sees human nature, penetrating its disguises and embracing all its force and weakness by that insight which is within him. . . .

" When the true poet or artist takes up in his hand a single garden pear or russet apple, he will behold, through its suggestions, as in a sorcerer's mirror, a whole smiling land of orchard and of meadow ; he will smell the sweet scent of ripe fruit and wet leaves ; he will tread a thousand grassy ways and wade in a thousand rippling streams ; he will hear the matin's bell and the evensong, the lowing kine and the bleating flocks ; he will think in a second of time of the trees which were in blossom when Drake and Raleigh sailed, and the fields which were green when the Tudor and Valois met, and the sunsets of long, long ago when Picardy was in the flames of war and all over the Norman lands the bowmen tramped and the fair knights rode.

" The phrasing of modern metaphysic calls this faculty assimilation ; in other days it has been called imagination : be its name what it will, it is the one essential and especial possession of the poetic mind, which makes it travel over space and annihilate time, and behold the endless life of innumerable forests as suggested to it by a single green leaf."

And in "Le Secret du Précepteur"[1] she sums up the "divers and numerous qualities" which must in her view be possessed by the creator of a fine novel : "Not only imagination but wit, not only wit but scholarship, not only scholarship but fancy, not only fancy but discrimination, observation, knowledge of the passions, sympathy with the most opposite temperaments, the power to call up character from the void, as the sculptor creates figures from the clay, and for amalgamating, condensing, and vivifying all these talents, the mastery of an exquisite subtlety, force, and eloquence in language." In continuation she implies that the reader who would properly appreciate the productions of such a novelist must possess almost similar qualities. It is difficult not to believe that Ouida was thinking of herself as the perfect novelist ; the power to call up character from the void she certainly possessed, and she would never have realized that such a power could not produce a great novelist.

Love and intrigue are her sole themes. Her characters exist only to make love and be made love to. Even if they have tangible work to do in the world, if they are painters or sculptors or musicians, directly

[1] Cf. *Critical Studies* (1900).

love touches them their work goes to the wall. Only
millionaires who have risen from the people seem able
to carry on their love affairs and their business at
the same time. She has scant faith in marriage,
because she thinks it absurd to expect a man worth
anything to be what she called "a hearth-bound
monogamist." Her women in love are either "splendidly" vicious or models of virtue, sacrificing everything for the sake of their usually worthless lovers
and dying when abandoned by them.

Of plot, in the artistic sense of the term, Ouida
was guiltless. She began by writing down everything
that came into her mind, descriptions, observations,
reflections, and then, when she had matter enough to
fill the book, ran a thread of story through it. In
most of her novels this method is easily traced ; in one
or two cases, however, she has paid more attention
to construction, but unfortunately, with the exception
of *In Maremma*, one of the best of the Italian
group of novels, this has generally happened
in her less attractive books, notably in *Moths*
and in *The Massarenes*, both lurid pictures of
nouveaux riches and the fast section of aristocratic
society.

In portrayal of character Ouida is generally deficient.
As a rule she draws a sort of flat design of the person
and fills it in with her own invention : we seldom
learn to know a character through his action. Among
her women characters, however, there are two excep-

tions : Cigarette [1] in *Under Two Flags* and Musa in *In Maremma*. They are consistent, and we do come to know them through what they do and say. Her men characters are not very attractive, although Ouida certainly intended them to be so. Wanderers like Tricotrin and Pascarèl, sculptors like Marys in *Ariadne*, or the old shoemaker who tells the story in that novel, have much to recommend them, and it is through such characters that we can trace Ouida's philosophy of life. The heroes of her earlier novels were the resplendent guardsmen so laughed at by later generations of novel-readers. Mr. G. S. Street characterizes the type as—

"A man of strong passions and a zeal for life. He grasps at the pleasures of life, and is eager for all its activities ; he will endure privations in the cause of sport, and discomforts in the cause of friendship, and risks in the cause of love . . . he is ready to fight and he does not swagger. His one affectation is, that if by chance he has done something great in the way of sport or war, he looks as if nothing had happened. There are things in life he puts before the main chance." [2]

That kind of man doubtless exists, though he is

---

[1] I was present last year at a performance of a dramatized version of *Under Two Flags* at the Lyceum Theatre, London, and, in accordance with my expectations, and in spite of the staginess and general melodramatic effects, the character of Cigarette stood out full of poetry, imagination, and tragedy.

[2] Cf. *The Yellow Book*, vol. vi.

rare, and it may be that some persons like to be reminded of him by the novelist, and are led thus to think better of life. Such heroes are to be found, not only in Ouida's novels, but in others equally popular as hers in their day and equally dead now, in *Guy Livingstone* and other of George Lawrence's novels, which undoubtedly greatly influenced Ouida's works, and in the soldiers and sportsmen who are the heroes of Whyte Melville's novels. Taste changes, ideals change, and such heroes were to novel-readers of the sixties and seventies of the nineteenth century what the heroes who renounce rank and pleasure and personal comfort to work among the poor and fallen in the slums of great cities are to the novel-readers of to-day. There is, perhaps, as little reality in the one type as portrayed in novels as in the other. Ouida's popularity in her time may be in some measure accounted for by the fact that there were and still are persons who have enough of the real in their workaday lives, and in their novels call for something outside and beyond it; who, indeed, like their novels to savour of the fairy-tale. But there is perhaps another reason. We must remember, as has been observed in a previous chapter, that the line of demarcation between classes was much stronger at the time of Ouida's great vogue; there was much more exclusiveness in high places than is the case now. Persons who were poor were looked down on by those who were rich. The middle class knew little except by hearsay of the doings and manner of life of the upper class. An Oxford professor would not in those degenerate days have been asked by the Prime Minister to meet the Sovereign at dinner, unless, perhaps, he had been a person of noble birth. Hence Ouida's portrayal of great folk and their ways would not have seemed absurd to the larger number of her readers. It would all have been unknown territory to them. They would have received it as gospel truth and have felt perfectly sure that they were being initiated into the mysteries of high life.

But many of Ouida's books possess qualities that make them attractive in spite of their many absurdities and inaccuracies. Whatever in them is meretricious and exaggerated, her love of beauty, whether it is to be found in nature or in art, her hatred of oppression and injustice, whether practised against man or beast, her sympathy with suffering in all forms, was genuine and sincere, however extravagant the terms in which she too often voiced her feelings.

Her best work is to be found in her Italian novels —I call them so because they are concerned with Italy—*Pascarèl* (1873), *Signa* (1875), *Ariadne* (1877), and *In Maremma* (1882). Other of her novels, as we shall see, deal with Italy, and contain much that is interesting and fine, but they fall below the level of these four.

In these novels Ouida has dealt almost exclusively with the Italian peasantry or the lower class of town-dwellers. As an example of her method let us briefly sketch the novel *Signa*. The scene is the district of Signa, near Florence, and the hero, the illegitimate son of a village girl and a French artist who later became famous, is called Signa after the place. So the name bears in the title a two-fold signification. Signa, the place, is worthy of knowledge ; Ouida knew it well, for the Villa Farinola was situated in that district.

"The years of its glory are done. It is a grey quiet place which now strays down by the water and now climbs high on the hill, and faces the full dawn of the day and sees the sunset reflected in the mirror of the river, and is starry with fire-flies in midsummer and at noon looks drowsy in the heat and seems to dream —being so very old. The buttressed walls are ruins. The mass-bell swings over the tower roofs. The fortresses are changed to farms. The vines climb where the culverins blazed. White bullocks and belled mules tread to and fro the tracks which the freelances made ; and the peasants sing at their ploughs where the hosts of the invaders once thundered.

"Its ways are narrow, its stones are crooked, its summer dust is dense, its winter mire is heavy, its hovels are many, its people are poor. Here where the ancient walls of its citadel rise hoary and broken against the blueness of the sky ; there where the arches of the bridges span the river, and the sand and the shallows and the straw that is drying in summer shine together yellow in the sun ; here, where under the sombre painted archways the little children play, their faces like the cherubs and the cupids of the Renaissance; there where the cobblers and coopers and the plaiting maidens and the makers of the yellow rush brooms all work away under the lintels, and corbels, and carved beam timbers, four hundred years old if one; here where through the gateways with their portcullises woven over by the spiders there only pass the patient mules with sacks of flour, or the hay carts dropping grasses, or the waggons of new wine; there where the villas that were all fortresses in the fierce fighting times of old gleam white in the light upon their crests of hills, with their cypresses like sentinels around them, and breadths of corn and vineyards traversed by green grassy paths that lead upward to where the stone-pine and the myrtle make sweet the air together. In all these Signa is beautiful; most of all, of course, in the long light, radiant summer, when the nightingales are singing everywhere, noon as well as night; the summer which seems to last almost all the year, for you can only tell how it comes and goes by the coming and going of the flowers; the long-lived summer that is ushered in by the daffodils, those golden chamberlains of the court of flowers, and dies, as a king should, on a purple bed of anemones, when the bells of the feast of the saints sound its requiem from hill to hill. And Signa revels in all the brightness of the Tuscan weather, and all about her seems singing, from the cicala piping away all day long, through the hottest heat, to the mandolines that thrill through the leaves at night as the peasants go by strumming the chords of their love-songs. Summer and song and sunshine ;—Signa lies amidst them like some war-bruised shield of a knight that has fallen amongst the roses and holds the nest of a lark."

It was Corpus Christi Day, and the people were chanting the Laus Deo, and above the voices rose one sweetest and clearest of all, that of a little ten-year-old boy, poorer than the rest, who lived with people who thrashed him oftener than they fed him. But music was in his head and in his heart. He had a little lute of his own, and he played and sang as he went along in the dusk of the dawn to his work. The child's music was wonderful in its way, but in Signa there was so much music everywhere that nobody noticed much.

" As the wine-waggon creaks down the hill, the waggoner will chaunt to the corn that grows upon either side of him. As the miller's mules cross the bridge, the lad as he cracks his whip will hum to the blowing alders. In the red clover, the labourers will whet their scythes and sickles to a trick of melody. In the quiet evenings a Kyrie Eleison will rise from the thick leaves that hide a village chapel. On the hills the goatherd, high in air amongst the arbutus branches, will scatter on the lonely mountain-side stanzas of purest rhythm. By the sea-shore, where Shelley died, the fisherman, rough and salt and weatherworn, will string notes of sweetest measure under the tamarisk-tree on his mandoline. But the poetry and the music float on the air like the leaves of roses that blossom in a solitude and drift away to die upon the breeze : there is no one to notice the fragrance, there is no one to gather the leaves."

The boy was the child of Pippa, the peasant girl who had run away with a French painter, Istriel. He deserted her, and returning to Signa at a time of flood, in a miserable condition, Pippa fell down a precipice and was killed, but the child, falling on her, was saved, and he and the woman's body were found by her brothers, Lippo and Bruno. Lippo had a wife and family, and he therefore agreed to take charge of the boy, while Bruno, who was unmarried, undertook to pay for the child's keep. The boy grew up and spent a good deal of time with Bruno, who came to love him and was almost jealous of the child's lute and of his love for Gemma, the gardener's daughter, a little girl of his own age. One day Bruno gave him some currants, and instead of eating them, in the evening he took them to Gemma. She had a sister a year older, named Palma. She was dark, and Gemma was fair. The children were already asleep on their bed of hay.

" 'I have brought you some fruit, Gemma,' he said, and tried to kiss her.

" 'Give me ! give me quick !' cried the little child. She pushed away his lips ; she wanted the fruit.

" 'If I do not eat it quick, Palma will wake,' she whispered, and began to crunch them in her tiny teeth as the kid did its grasses. The dark child did wake, and lifted herself on her elbow.

" 'It is Signa !' she cried, with a little coo of delight like a wood-pigeon's.

" 'I kept you no currants, Palma !' said Signa, with a sudden pang of self-reproach. He knew that he had done unkindly.

" Palma looked a little sorrowful. They were very poor, and never hardly tasted anything except the black bread like the dogs.

" 'Never mind ; come and kiss me,' she said, with a little sigh.

" Signa went round and kissed her. But he went back to Gemma again.

" 'Good night,' he said to the pretty white child sitting up in the hay ; and he kissed her once more. So Gemma was kissed twice, and had the currants as well.

" Palma was used to that.

" Signa ran out with a hardened conscience. He knew he had been unjust ; but then if he had given any of the currants to Palma, Gemma never would have kissed him at all.

" They were both his play-fellows, but Palma he did not care about, and about Gemma he did. For Gemma was a thousand times the prettier, and Palma loved him always, that he knew ; but of Gemma he never was so sure."

Ouida as Novelist

I quote this passage at length because it strikes the keynote of Ouida's attitude to women and shows her fixed idea, one that prevails throughout her work, that the selfish, unscrupulous women are those whom men love best.

Signa grew up, loving and making music as he could. The organist of the little church taught him much. Signa loved all beautiful things, too, and one day Bruno took him to the Certosa to see the "marble men and painted angels." There he met a stranger, a French painter, who, hearing him sing, was so delighted with his voice and his beauty that he painted his head and made him a present of 40 francs, with which Signa bought an old violin he had longed for for ages. Lippo, who persistently ill-treated the boy, was furiously angry that the money had not been given to him, and Signa determined to run away and persuaded Gemma to go with him. Signa played his violin and sang and Gemma danced. The leader of a travelling mountebank show happened to witness their performance and enticed the children to accompany him to Leghorn, intending to take ship there. But before they got off, Bruno found them. Gemma, however, vanished while Signa and Bruno left her to rest at an inn under the care of the landlady.

Then Signa went to live with Bruno, and Bruno worked and saved for him, and Signa was happy in the purely agricultural life he led.

" In the country of Virgil, life remains pastoral still. A certain peace and light lie on the people at their toil. The reaper with his hook, the plougher with his oxen, the girl who gleans amongst the trailing vines, the child that sees the flowers tossing with the corn, the men that sing to get a blessing on the grapes —they have all a certain grace and dignity of the old classic ways left with them."

It was a peaceful, wholesome life, full of labour it is true, but labour out in the open fields under blue skies ; and Signa found time, too, in which, under the old organist, he could pursue his music. He grew into a handsome youth. And the time came when Bruno explained to him that the result of his toil was that Signa would have a good deal of land all his own, and in due time—he was now seventeen— could marry and become a rich contadino. But Signa cared for none of these things. He wanted to go to Florence and study music, and Bruno in his disappointment broke the youth's violin.

" ' I hate him,' said Signa. ' Palma, see here. He pretends to love me, and he breaks my Rusignuola, and he breaks my heart with it, and he thinks he loves me, both body and soul, because he buys a bit of land and bids me live on it all the days of my life, and dig, and sow, and plough, and hew, and draw water, and lead a life like the oxen's—no better : he calls that love.' "

Palma took a different view.

" ' Bruno has been so good, and given up so much and hoped so much : is it not just a little hard that you should be so longing to leave him ? Perhaps he does love you selfishly. But is not your want to get away selfish too ? He has been cruel. Oh, yes ! that is certain. But then no doubt he was in pain : he hardly knew what he did.' "

Bruno repented, and sent Signa to Bologna to study music. And later sold the land, the very land he had bought for Signa, so that he might have the 3,000 francs required to have the opera *Actæa* that he had composed produced in Venice. It was a great success ; Signa awoke and found himself famous. And then he met again the Gemma of his childhood, now a beautiful wicked woman, a shameless wanton, living under the protection of Istriel, the painter, who was of course Signa's father. And she ensnares Signa and then deceives him, and so brings him to his death. The character of Bruno is finely and consistently drawn ; he gives up everything for his beloved nephew, even his life, for it was he who killed Gemma, though all too late, since Signa had discovered her faithlessness and had slain himself. As Bruno went to the scaffold, he said in his heart, " I did what I could. But it was all of no use—of no use ! " There is real tragedy in the climax, and it is well led up to.

Rome is really the subject of *Ariadne*. True, there is the usual thread of story, which portrays the sufferings of an innocent loving girl caused by the cruel treatment of a worldly, egotistical lover. But we read the book for its delightful Roman setting.

Here is one picture :—

" Water is the living joy of Rome.

" I wonder to hear them say that Rome is sad, with all that mirth and music of its water laughing through all its streets, till the steepest and stoniest ways are murmurous with it as any brook-fed forest depths. Here water is Protean ; sovereign and slave, sorcerer and servant, slaking the mule's thirst and shining in porphyry on the prince's terrace, filling the well in the cabbage-garden and leaping aloft against the Pope's palace ; first called to fill the baths of the Agrippines and serve the Naumachia of Augustus, it bubbles from a griffin's jaws or a wolf's teeth, or any other of the thousand quaint things set in the masonry at street corners, and washes the people's herbs and carrots, and is lapped by the tongues of dogs, and thrashed by the bare brown arms of washing women ; first brought from the hills to flood the green Numidian marble of the thermæ, and lave the limbs of the patricians between the cool mosaic walls of the tepidarium, it contentedly becomes a household thing, twinkling like a star at the bottom of deep old wells in dusky courts, its rest broken a dozen times a day by the clash of the chain on the copper pail, above it the carnations of the kitchen balcony and the caged blackbird of the cook.

" One grows to love the Roman fountains as sea-

born men love the sea. Go where you will there is
water ; whether it foams by Trevi, where the green
moss grows in it like ocean weed about the feet of the
ocean-god, or whether it rushes reddened by the
evening light from the mouth of an old lion that
once saw Cleopatra ; whether it leaps high in air trying
to reach the gold cross on St. Peter's, or pours its
triple cascade over the Pauline granite ; whether it
spouts out of a great barrel in a wall in old Trastevere,
or throws up into the air a gossamer as fine as
Arachne's web in a green garden way where the
lizards run, or in a crowded corner where the fruit-
sellers sit against the wall—in all its shapes one grows
to love the water that fills Rome with an unchanging
melody all through the year."

And where is the charm of a student's life in Rome
more romantically brought out than in this description ?—

"There can be hardly any life more lovely upon
earth than that of a young student of art in Rome.
With the morning, to rise to the sound of countless
bells and of innumerable streams, and see the silver
lines of the snow new fallen on the mountains against
the deep rose of the dawn, and the shadows of the
night steal away softly from off the city, releasing, one
by one, dome and spire, and cupola and roof, till all
the wide white wonder of the place reveals itself
under the broad brightness of full day ; to go down
into the dark cool streets, with the pigeons fluttering in

the fountains, and the sounds of the morning chants
coming from many a church door and convent
window, and little scholars and singing children going
by with white clothes on, or scarlet robes, as though
walking forth from the canvas of Botticelli or
Garofalo ; to eat frugally, sitting close by some shop
of flowers and birds, and watching all the while the
humours and the pageants of the streets by quaint
corners, rich with sculptures of the Renaissance, and
spanned by arches of architects that builded for
Agrippa, under grated windows with arms of
Frangipani or Colonna, and pillars that Apollodorus
raised ; to go into the great courts of palaces,
murmurous with the fall of water, and fresh with
green leaves and golden fruit, that rob the colossal
statues of their gloom and gauntness, and thence into
the vast chambers where the greatest dreams that
men have ever had are written on panel and on canvas,
and the immensity and the silence of them all are
beautiful and eloquent with dead men's legacies to the
living, where the Hours and the Seasons frolic beside
the Maries at the Sepulchre, and Adonis bares his
lovely limbs, in nowise ashamed because St. Jerome
and St. Mark are there ; to study and muse, and
wonder and be still, and be full of the peace which
passes all understanding, because the earth is lovely as
Adonis is, and life is yet unspent ; to come out of the
sacred light, half golden, and half dusky, and full of
many blended colours, where the marbles and the

pictures live, sole dwellers in the deserted dwellings of princes ; to come out where the oranges are all aglow in the sunshine, and the red camellias are pushing against the hoary head of the old stone Hermes, and to go down the width of the mighty steps into the gay piazza, alive with bells tolling, and crowds laughing, and drums a-beat, and the flutter of carnival banners in the wind ; and to get away from it all with a full heart, and ascend to see the sun set from the terrace of the Medici, or the Pamfili, or the Borghese woods, and watch the flame-like clouds stream homewards behind St. Peter's, and the pines of Monte Mario grow black against the west, till the pale green of the evening spreads itself above them, and the stars arise ; and then, with a prayer—be your faith what it will—a prayer to the Unknown God, to go down again through the violet-scented air and the dreamful twilight, and so,—with unspeakable thankfulness, simply because you live, and this is Rome,—so homeward."

In *Pascarèl* again the story is slight and not particularly interesting, but the picture it gives of Italy in Garibaldian days is admirable. Pascarèl himself, a strolling player, is a breezy, whimsical, and very attractive person. Nearly every place in Tuscany is described or mentioned, and both its past and present aspects touched on. Very often an illuminating sentence, such as "Pisa, the ruined rival of Florence—the old city sad and sombre with Orcagna's

death," occurs, and among the cities through which
Pascarèl and his troupe pass are Cremona, Assisi,
Ferrara, Urbino, Pistoia, Arezzo, Genoa, Mantua,
Florence being his headquarters. He delights in
his land, and is almost a poet when he describes
her beauty and her charm. Here is a picture of
spring in Italy, the truth and beauty of which will
be recognised by all who have witnessed that season
there :—

"There is nothing upon earth, I think, like the
smile of Italy as she awakes when the winter has dozed
itself away in the odours of its oakwood fires.

" The whole land seems to laugh.

" The springtide of the north is green and beautiful,
but it has nothing of the radiance, the dreamfulness,
the ecstasy of spring in the southern countries. The
springtide of the north is pale with the gentle, colourless sweetness of its world of primroses ; the springtide of Italy is rainbow-hued, like the profusion of
anemones that laugh with it in every hue of glory
under every ancient wall and beside every hill-fed
stream.

" Spring in the north is a child that wakes from
dreams of death ; spring in the south is a child that
wakes from dreams of love. One is rescued and welcomed from the grave ; but the other comes smiling
on a sunbeam from heaven.

  .   .   .   .   .

" Come out here in the young months of summer

and leave the highways that grim walls fence in, and
stray through the field-paths and the bridle-roads in the
steps of the contadini, and you will find this green
world about your feet touched with the May-day suns
to tenderest and most lavish wealth of nature.

"The green corn uncurling underneath the blossoming vines. The vine foliage that tosses and climbs and
coils in league on league of verdure. The breast-high
grasses full of gold and red and purple from the
countless flowers growing with it.

"The millet filled with crimson gladioli and great
scarlet poppies. The hill-sides that look a sheet of
rose-colour where the lupinelli are in bloom. The tall
plumes of the canes, new-born, by the side of every
stream and rivulet.

"The sheaves of arum leaves that thrust themselves
out from every joint of masonry or spout of broken
fountain. The flame of roses that burns on every
handsbreadth of untilled ground and springs like a
rainbow above the cloud of every darkling roof or
wall. The ocean spray of arbutus and acacia shedding
its snow against the cypress darkness. The sea-green
of the young ilex leaves scattered like light over the
bronze and purple of the older growth. The dreamy
blue of the iris lilies rising underneath the olives and
along the edges of the fields.

"The soft, pretty, quiet pictures where mowers sweep
down with their scythes the reedy grasses on the river
banks ; where the gates of the villas stand wide open

with the sun aslant upon the grassy paths and the vines;
where in the gloom of the house archways the women
sit plaiting their straw, the broad, shining fields before
them all alive with the song of the grilli ; where the
grey, savage walls of a fortress tower on the spur of
the mountains, above the delicate green of young oaks
and the wind-stirred fans of the fig-trees ; where the
frate, in broad-leaved hat of straw, brushes with bare
sandalled feet through the bright acanthus, beaming a
Rabelaisian smile on the contadina who goes by him
with her brown water-jar upon her head ; where deep
in that fresh, glad tumult of leaf and blossom and
bough the children and the goats lie together, while the
wild-thyme and the trefoil are in flower, and the little
dog-rose is white amongst the maize ; where the sharp
beak of the galley-like boat cuts dark against the yellow
current, and the great, filmy square nets are cast outward
where the poplar shadows tremble in the stream ; all
these, and a thousand like them, are yours in the sweet
May season amongst the Tuscan hills and vines."

And here is a picture of summer :—

" No northern landscape can ever have such inter-
change of colour as the Italian fields and hills in
summer. Here the fresh vine foliage, hanging,
curling, climbing, in all intricacies and graces that ever
entered the fancies of green leaves. There the tall
millet, towering like the plumes of warriors, whilst
among their stalks the golden lizard glitters. Here
broad swaths of new-mown hay, starred over with

butterflies of every hue. There a thread of water sown thick with waving canes. Here the shadowy amber of ripe wheat, rustled by wind and darkened by passing clouds. There the gnarled olives silver in the sun. And everywhere along the edges of the corn and underneath the maples little grassy paths running, and wild rose bushes growing, and acacia thickets tossing, and white convolvulus glistening like snow, and across all this confusion of foliage and herbage always the tender, dreamy swell of the far mountains.

.　　.　　.　　.　　.

"Do you know the delicate delights of a summer morning in Italy ?—morning, I mean, between four and five of the clock.

"The nights, perfect as they are, have scarcely more loveliness than the birth of light, the first rippling laughter of the early day.

"The air is cool, almost cold, and clear as glass. There is an endless murmur from birds' throats and wings, and from far away there will ring from village or city the chimes of the first mass. The deep broad shadows lie so fresh, so grave, so calm, that by them the very dust is stilled and spiritualized.

"Softly the sun comes, striking first the loftier trees and then the blossoming magnolias, and lastly the green lowliness of the gentle vines ; until all above is in a glow of new-born radiance, whilst all beneath the leaves still is dreamily dusk and cool.

"The sky is of a soft sea-blue ; great vapours will

float here and there, iris-coloured and snow-white. The stone parapets of bridge and tower shine against the purple of the mountains, which are low in tone, and look like hovering storm-clouds. Across the fields dun oxen pass to their labours ; through the shadows peasants go their way to mass ; down the river a raft drifts slowly, with the pearly waters swaying against the canes ; all is clear, tranquil, fresh as roses washed with rain."

A description of Florence as seen from Galileo's Tower is worth quoting :—

"Very fair indeed she was, the Lily Queen, that evening.

"There had been shadows all day, and in the west there were masses of cloud, purple and blue-black, spreading away into a million of soft scarlet cirri that drifted before a low wind from the southward, tender and yet rich in tone as any scattered shower of carnation leaves.

"Through that vast pomp of dusky splendour and that radiance of rose the sun itself still shone ; shone full upon the city.

"Leaning on the broken edge of the watch-tower and gazing down below, all Florence seemed like the seer's dream of the New Jerusalem ; every stone of her seemed transmuted ; she was as though paven and built with gold ; straightway across the whole valley stretched the alchemy of that wondrous fireglow, and all the broad, level lands of the Valdigreve were transfigured likewise into one vast sheet of gold, on which the silver olives and the dim white villages and villas floated like frail white sails upon a sunlit sea.

"Farther—still farther yet, beyond that burnished ocean—the mountains and the clouds met and mingled, golden likewise, broken here and there into some tenderest rose-leaf flush, miraculously lovely, as a poet's dreams of nameless things of God.

"We stayed long, and watched it high above on the wooden roof of the Tower ; watched it until the sun had set, and the glow had died, and the stillness of evening had fallen over the hills and plains, and past our faces flew a little grey downy owl."

In Pascarèl's disquisitions on the Italian people we may not unfairly see Ouida's own estimation of them :—

"As for the people—the dear people !—the more I dwelt amongst them the more I loved them. There is no other people on the face of the earth so entirely lovable, even with their many faults, as the Italians. But what is known of them by other nations ?—hardly anything at all.

"That the Italian patrician may be little understood outside the pale of his own immediate associates, it is not difficult to conceive. His confidence is rarely bestowed ; and the pride which fences him in is at once the most delicate and the most impenetrable that a man can place betwixt himself and the outer world.

"But it is passing strange that the Italian popolano, open to whosoever will to study him at their leisure, the

Italian of the people, as seen in his streets and fields, by his hearth, and his market stall, is as little understood and as invariably misrepresented.

"French vivacity and ease have passed into a proverb; yet, in reality, the French people are studied and conscious compared to the Italian, who is the most absolutely unstudied and unselfconscious of all God's creatures.

"True, the Italian, even in the lowest strata of social life, has a repose and a dignity in him which befit his physiognomy and evince themselves in his calm and poetical attitudes. See a stonebreaker, or a mason, or a boatman asleep in the noonday sun, and you will surely see attitudes which no sculptor could wish bettered for his marble.

"True, too, you will do ill to make a mock of him; high or low, it is the one unpardonable sin which no Italian will pardon; he is given also to the immovable obstinacy of that animal which he will never name save under the delicate euphuism of 'the little black gentleman'; and he has a lightning-like passion in him which may smite his neighbour to the earth in a trice about a cherry-stone, or a broken broom, or any other *casus belli* of the hour.

"But, then, lo! how bright he is, how gregarious, how neighbourly, how instant and graceful in courtesy, how eager and kindly in willingness; how poetic his glee in song and dance, and holy day and pageant; how absolute his content upon the most meagre fare that ever held body and soul together ; how certain his invariable selection of a pleasure for the eye and the ear, rather than one for the mouth and the stomach !

"See the gay, elastic grace of him ; the mirth that ripples all day long about him like the sunlight, the laughter that shows his white teeth, the tumultuous shouts in which his lungs delight, the cheery sociability that brings him with a knot of his own kind at the street corners and under the house archways to talk the hours away with tireless tongue and shrewdest wit, and say, is there a creature kindlier or more mirthful anywhere in the width of the world ?

"And he will always have some delicate touch of the artist in him, too, and always some fine instinct of the gentleman—let him be poor as he will, ill-clad, half-starved, and ignorant even of the letters that make his name ; let him feel the summer dust with bare feet, and the mountain wind through a ragged shirt, nay, let him be the veriest scamp and sinner in the world—but he will wear his tatters with a grace ; he will bring a flower to a woman with the bow of a king ; and he will resent an insolence with an air to which no purple and fine linen could lend dignity."

And lastly let us hear Pascarèl on his own art :—

"What is it to be a player ? It is this. A thing despised and rejected on all sides ; a thing that was a century since denied what they call Christian burial; a thing that is still deemed for a woman disgraceful and for a man degrading and emasculate ; a thing that is mute as a dunce save when, parrot-like, it repeats by rote with a mirthless grin or a tearless sob ; a wooden doll, as you say, applauded as a brave puppet in its prime, hissed at in its first hour of failure or decay ; a thing made up of tinsel and paint, and patchwork, of the tailor's shreds and the barber's curls of tow—a ridiculous thing, to be sure ! That is a player. And yet again—a thing without which laughter and jest were dead in the sad lives of the populace ; a thing that breathes the poet's words of fire so that the humblest heart is set aflame ; a thing that has a magic on its lips to waken smiles or weeping at its will ; a thing which holds a people silent, breathless, intoxicated with mirth or with awe, as it chooses ; a thing whose grace kings envy, and whose wit great men will steal ; a thing by whose utterance alone the poor can know the fair follies of a thoughtless hour, and escape for a little space from the dull prisons of their colourless lives into the sunlit paradise where genius dwells ;—*that* is a player, too ! "

There is food for thought here. The passage calls to mind a fine speech in the little one-act drama entitled *Comedy and Tragedy*, written by W. S. Gilbert for Miss Mary Anderson in 1884.

In other of Ouida's novels the scene is partly or wholly laid in Italy. But where, as in *In a Winter City* and in *Friendship*, the story is one of modern life in a narrow aristocratic section of society, the Italian setting is less telling, and the persons portrayed might have lived their little romances or practised their wickedness in London or New York or Paris, equally well. But even in them descriptive pieces of great charm are not lacking. For example :—

"The San Cipriano was to be found in a church some five miles out of the city;[1] a lonely church set high on a fragrant hill-side, with sheep amongst the olive boughs, and the ox-plough under the vines that were all about it, and high hedges of wild roses and thickets of arbutus rambling around its old walled graveyard. . . . It was one of those spring days which often fall in February ; the ground was blue with violets, and the grass golden with crocus and hepatica ; there were butterflies and bees on the air ; the mavis and the blackbird were singing."[2]

Here is a scrap of conversation that illuminates the love of nature among the Southern peoples of Europe, and also shows the different way in which the Northern races care for external nature :—

" 'People think Horace's love of the rural life an affectation. I believe it to be most sincere. After the strain of the conventionality and the adulation of the Augustan Court, the natural existence of the country must have been welcome to him. I know it is the fashion to say that a love of nature belongs only to the moderns, but I do not think so. Into Pindar, Theocritus, Meleager, the passion for nature must have

[1] Florence.   [2] From *In a Winter City*.

entered very strongly ; what is modern is the more subjective, the more fanciful, feeling which makes nature a sounding-board to echo a.l the cries of man.'

" ' But that is always a Northern feeling ? '

" ' Inevitably. With us nature is too *riante* for us to grow morbid about it. The sunshine that laughs around us nine months of every year, the fruits that grow almost without culture, the flowers that we throw to the oxen to eat, the very stones that are sweet with myrtle, the very sea sand that is musical with bees in the rosemary, everything we grow up amongst from infancy makes our love of nature only a kind of unconscious joy in it—but here even the peasant has that, and the songs of the men that cannot read or write are full of it. If a field labourer sing to his love he will sing of the narcissus and the crocus.' " [1]

Vernon Lee, who knows Italy even better than Ouida knew it, has paid high tribute to Ouida's descriptions of Italy, and her words may fitly conclude the estimate of them I have here attempted to give :—

" Italy—perhaps every great country—has so many possible appeals to the soul that a new one requires to be made every generation or two, and the Treasure-house to be opened by successive sayers of 'Sesame.' After the Italy of Goethe, of Byron, of Alfred de Musset, and George Sand (let alone Ruskin's !) ; and before that of Pater ; perhaps some will add of Mr. Hewlett—comes the Italy of Browning and of

[1] From *In a Winter City.*

Ouida as Novelist

Ouida. I do not hesitate to couple these two names, for I am speaking not of the work itself, which in Browning's case will probably be enduring, and in Ouida's is already rather obsolete, but of the effect on the contemporary reader's mind. *Signa*, *Ariadne*, the enchanting *Pascarèl*, have given us not less than the *Ring and the Book* and *Men and Women* an Italy which was unknown before, and which, once revealed, will never be lost again."

Vernon Lee also finds that Ouida's Italian novels have influenced those of Mrs. Wharton, that Ouida may be found in the admirable pages about Italy by Maurice Barrès and Mme. de Noailles, and in the mediæval fantasies of Anatole France, and she vehemently declares that there is Ouida at every step in the prose of D'Annunzio, and that in his work there is the permeating, emotional, and imaginative atmosphere, the golden dust-cloud of past greatness, which makes a halo round every one of Ouida's Italian personages.[1]

To these authors I should be inclined to add three or four contemporary English novelists who consciously or unconsciously owe much to Ouida.

Ouida showed much skill in the writing of short stories. She possessed something of the art that belongs in that genre supremely to French writers. The tales that deal with Italian peasant life or with dogs are admirable, and it would be worth while to

---

[1] Cf. *Westminster Gazette*, July 27, 1907.

rescue a dozen of the best of them from the oblivion into which they have undeservedly fallen, and print them in one volume. She repeats her themes, it is true, but the setting is always delightful, and, compelled to work in a restricted space, she keeps within bounds and evolves a more artistic whole than she ever accomplishes in her longer novels. Ouida herself regarded such tales as *A Dog of Flanders*, *Two Offenders*, *Santa Barbara*, as her finest and most finished work. She often said to her friend Sarmento : "The short tale is to prose what the sonnet is to poetry—the highest form of art." In the stories in which dogs play the chief part the quality of the work is indubitably very high. I have only met the same sympathy with the animal's point of view in the writings of Maeterlinck and those of the accomplished French writer, Louis Pergaud.

Ouida's English style cannot be praised. It has been well said that "she has not a command of language, but language has a command of her." She always writes well when she writes of Italy, and the passages quoted in this chapter will serve to show her style at its best. It became more restrained and more simple in the later years of her life, and good writing is to be found in the *Critical Studies*, and in the letters to her friends. The grave defect of the inaccuracy of her historical, literary, and geographical allusions, due to carelessness rather than to ignorance, has already been pointed out.

Ouida as Novelist

Her power of assimilation and of absorbing and reproducing local colour is her chief claim to genius, and, take of her work in general what view we may, her Italian novels, some of her short stories and of her critical essays deserve a permanent place on our bookshelves among the lesser writers of the Victorian era.

Mr. Wilfrid Scawen Blunt takes a higher estimate of her novels, and I print here the words he has specially written for this book :—

"Though no indiscriminate admirer of Ouida's novels, I had and have a high opinion of the best of them as works of genius. In spite of their exaggerations and occasional absurdities of detail, I hold them to be the only English novels which can at all be compared with Balzac's as giving a vivid and life-like picture of the larger world of society, women as well as men, they describe. Neither Thackeray, Balzac's nearest English rival in fiction, nor Meredith, nor any other as far as I know of our mid-Victorian novelists who went to the *beau monde* for their models succeeded as well as Ouida did in giving us the true social atmosphere and in making their men, and especially their women, act and live. Thackeray's women were little more than lay figures, and Meredith's, though interesting as studies of what women might be, very seldom display them as doing what women really do. Ouida's women, on the contrary, even in their extreme of caricature, are all

273   S

true to type, and easily recognizable as existing personalities. They have life and reality and individual interest. Her range, too, of subjects is, like Balzac's, very wide, and she is still more at home in Continental Europe than in England. No better description of Italy in its romantic aspect of the Garibaldian age exists in English literature than her novel *Pascarèl*. I remember discussing Ouida's merits on this head with Auberon Herbert some twenty years ago, and finding that his view of them was much the same as mine. He had had the reviewing of many of her novels, he told me, and had conceived for them a high respect."

VIII

OUIDA
AS CRITIC

CHAPTER VIII

OUIDA AS CRITIC

OUIDA was in the habit throughout her life of expressing her opinions with great vehemence in her books, in her letters and articles in the Press, and in private letters to her friends on all matters that passed before her in which she was interested. It must be confessed that her principles of criticism did not necessarily coincide with the principles that guided her own life. But this does not prevent her from being at times a very acute critic both of men and matters. It is often much easier to judge correctly of others than to judge wisely for ourselves. If we read straight through all Ouida's essays in criticism, we shall at first come to the conclusion that her opinions are merely a mass of contradictions, and so of little or no worth. But when we eliminate the purely personal element and begin to look beneath the surface, we see that her judgments are discriminating and full of good sense. Her essays have been collected in two volumes : *Views and Opinions* (1895) and *Critical Studies* (1900), of which the latter is by far the more important. But some of her best pieces of criticism are to be found in her private letters, as readers of the preceding chapters will have observed. Her judgment ripened in later years, and, though her utterances were usually coloured by her personal prejudices, they are always worth careful attention.

In her youth Ouida was a great reader of good literature, and especially of the works of the older writers, both French and English. Later on she seems to have confined her reading to contemporary literature, chiefly to *belles lettres*, with a few books on history and on social questions written by those with whose point of view she agreed.

Critical passages of worth abound in her novels. Here is an admirable comparison of Shakespeare and Dante :—

" Can you read Shakespeare ? You think Dante greater ? Of course you do, being an Italian. But you are wrong. Dante never got out of his own narrow world. He filled the great blank of Hereafter with his own spites and despites. He marred his finest verse with false imagery to rail at a foe or flaunt a polemic. His Eternity was only a millpond in which he should be able to drown the dogs he hated. A great man !—ah, yes !—but never by a league near Shakespeare. Sympathy is the hall-mark of the poet. Genius should be wide as the heavens and deep as the sea in infinite comprehension. To understand intuitively—that is the breath of its life. Whose understanding was ever as boundless as Shakespeare's? From the woes of the mind diseased to the coy joys of the yielding virgin; from the ambitions of the king and the conqueror to the clumsy glee of the clown and the milkmaid; from the highest heights of human life to the lowest follies of it—he comprehended all. That is the wonder of Shakespeare. No other writer was ever so miraculously impersonal. . . . He had only a witty smile at false dignities, and a matchless universality of compassion that pitied the tyrant as well as the serf, and the loneliness of royalty as well as the loneliness of poverty. That is where Shakespeare is unapproachable. He is as absolutely impartial as a Greek Chorus. . . . If it were the impartiality of coldness, it would be easy to imitate; but it is the impartiality of sympathy, boundless and generous as the sun, which 'shines upon the meanest thing that lives as liberally as on the summer rose.' That is where Shakespeare is as far higher from your Dante as one of Dante's angels from the earth." [1]

Here again are some wise reflections on progress and the difference between youth and age, put into the mouth of a great and successful sculptor :—

"Surely the world, made up of human beings as it is, is only like one human being in his passage through life. To youth belong ineffable graces all its own, and charms never to be counterfeited when youth has passed away; hope and faith and the freshness of unbroken

[1] *Ariadne.*

illusions are with it; it has the bloom as of the un-
touched fruit, the charm as of the half-opened flower;
it is rich in the treasures of its untried years, and strong
in the insolence of its beauty and its strength; it is
without suspicion and without fear; but, also, it is
without sympathy; it is glorious as the glory of the
morning, but he who seeks its pity finds it hard, from
pure joyousness of soul and ignorance of sorrow; its
selfishness is only ignorance, but it is selfish; it says to
every passing hour, 'Thou art fair,' why should it look
elsewhere? When youth is gone, the character that
has gained from living any profit will have softened
and mellowed under the suns and storms of many
days; with wide experience it will have wide toleration
and comprehension; its sympathies will be unfailing,
because it will be aware that 'to understand is to
pardon,' since for all evil there is excuse, could all
influences and motives and accidents of circumstance
be traced; its own past lies behind it, a land for ever
lost, and its onward path is dark; it looks back so
often because it hath not heart to look forward, since
all it sees is death; many are the graves of its desires
and of its friends; it is full of pity for all things that
breathe, because it has learned that nearly every breath
is pain; there is nothing in which it can have much
belief, but there is little to which it can refuse compassion, since all creation suffers; the unutterable
sadness and mystery of all forms of life oppress it, and
it hears the children and the lovers say, 'For ever,'

knowing itself too well that the mortal's 'for ever' is but the gnat's day upon a ray of sun and breath of vapour.

"As thus with the individual character of man, so it is with the character of the world and of those arts in which the voice of the world's soul speaks.

"Fearlessness, loveliness, and force characterized all that it did and all that it sang of in an earlier time; tenderness and pity are the excellences of all the best that it produces now. In the first ages all achievement and inspiration were fresh as the dews of dawn, and he who struck the lyre had no fear that his hymns were but weak echoes of a stronger sound. All was new, all was spontaneous. Now all this is changed. We feel that our production can hardly ever be more than repetition. . . .

"But if we have lost the force and the freshness of an earlier day, we have gained something else not wholly to be despised.

"I think that while we have, perhaps, lost dignity, and certainly have lost concentration, our sight is more extended, our range of feeling more varied, our understanding of pain and of joy more acute. . . .

"This world of our own immediate day is weak and weary, because it is no longer young; yet it possesses one noble attribute—it has an acute and almost universal sympathy, which does indeed often degenerate into a false and illogical sentiment, yet serves to redeem an age of egotism. We have escaped both the gem-like hardness of the Pagan and the narrowing selfishness of the Christian and the Israelite. We are sick for the woe of creation, and we wonder why such woe is ours, and why it is entailed on the innocent dumb beasts that perish in millions for us, unpitied, day and night. Rome had no altar to pity : it is the one god that we own. When that pity in us for all things is perfected, perhaps we shall have reached a religion of sympathy that will be purer than any religion the world has yet seen, and more productive. 'Save my country!' cried the Pagan to his deities. 'Save my soul!' cries the Christian at his altars. We, who are without a god, murmur to the great unknown forces of Nature : 'Let me save others some little portion of this pain entailed on all simple and guileless things that are forced to live, without any fault of their own at their birth, or any will of their own in their begetting.'" [1]

The collection of essays entitled *Views and Opinions* is dedicated to W. H. Mallock "as a slight token of personal regard and intellectual admiration." They are short pieces mostly on social subjects. Among them, however, there is an excellent essay on Shelley, and another on Pierre Loti's *Le Livre de la Pitié et de la Mort*, entitled " Death and Pity." The latter contains appreciative criticism of Loti's work, but Ouida admires him chiefly for the love and understanding of

[1] *Ariadne.*

animals that is shown in all his books. " He does prove, and has ever proved, in his conduct as in his writings, that to him nothing human can be alien. But he is not hemmed in behind the narrow pale of humanitarianism ; he has the vision to see, and the courage to show, that the uncounted, sentient, suffering children of creation for whom humanity has no mercy, but merely servitude and slaughter, are as dear to him as his own kind."

Several causes drew Ouida to Shelley : his love of Italy, and the fine expression of it in his poems ; the criticism of his way of life by what she calls English middle-class opinion ; his hatred of tyranny and his pity for pain. She considered him to be more truly a son of Italy than any one of her own poets, and declared that neither Shelley nor Byron could be well comprehended by those not intimately acquainted with Italian landscape. "Every line in Shelley's verse which speaks of Italy is pregnant with the spirit of the land. Each line is a picture ; true and perfect, whether of day or night, of water or shore, of marsh or garden, of silence or melody." She especially points to the Venetian setting of " Julian and Maddalo," a delight to all who have known Venice and loved her, to the scene of the "Epipsychidion," which "though called Greek, is Italian, and might be taken from the woods beside the Lake of Garda, or the Serchio, which he knew so well, or the forest-like parks which lie deep and cool and still in the blue shadows of Apennine or

Abruzzi." There is good criticism of the " Ode to
the West Wind," in every line of which Ouida says
" we feel the sweep and motion of the strong *libeccio*
coming from the grey Atlantic. When that wind
sweeps up the broad bed of the Arno, the yellowing
canebrakes bend, the rushes thrill and tremble, the
summer's empty nests are shaken from the ilex and
oak boughs, the great pines bend and tremble, the
river, stirred by the breath of the sea, grows yellow
and grey and swollen and turgid, the last swallow flies
southward from his home under the eaves of granary
or chapel, and the nightingales rise from their haunts
in the thickets of laurel and bay and go also where the
shadows of Indian temples or of Egyptian palm-trees
lie upon the sands of a still older world." Ouida
declares Shelley's supreme glory to be that beyond
all others he went where " no keel ever ploughed
before," and dwelt more completely than any other
has ever dwelt

> " On an imagined shore
> Where the gods spoke with him."

With Apollo in the " Prometheus Unbound " Shelley
might say—

> " And I shall gaze not on deeds which make
> My mind obscure with sorrow, as eclipse
> Darkens the sphere I guide ; but list, I hear
> The small, clear, silver lute of the young Spirit
> That sits i' the morning star."

284

And she concludes a fine essay that deserves to be better known with the words :—

"If ever poet held that lute on earth, Shelley held it all through his brief life ; and if ever there be immortality for any soul, his surely is living now beside that Spirit in the light of a ceaseless day.

> "'Death is the veil which those who live call life ;
> They sleep, and it is lifted.'"

Ouida was wholly against woman suffrage and against the "new woman," as the phrase went in the last decade of the nineteenth century. Two essays in this volume express her views, and beneath the vehement language is much sound sense. She inveighed against the vulgarity of the age, and showed in many essays how the materialistic spirit vulgarized not only places but peoples. In an article entitled "Vulgarity" occurs the following delightful description of a well-bred woman, in which Ouida is at her best :—

"I once knew a perfectly well-bred person who yet could neither read nor write. I can see her now in her little cottage in the Derbyshire woods on the brown, flashing water of the Derwent River (Darron, as the people of Derbyshire call it), a fair, neat, stout old woman with a round face and a clean mob-cap. She had been a factory girl in her youth (indeed, all her womanhood had worked at the cotton-mill on the river), and now was too old to do anything except to keep her one-roomed cottage, with its tall lancet windows, its peaked red roof, and its sweet-smelling garden, with its high elder hedge, as neat and fresh and clean as human hands could make them. Dear old Mary! with her racy, Chaucerian English, and her happy, cheerful temper, and her silver spectacles, which some of the 'gentry' had given her, and her big Bible on the little round table, and the black kettle boiling in the wide fireplace, and her casements wide open to the nodding moss-roses and the sweetbrier boughs! Dear old Mary! she was a bit of Shakespeare's England, of Milton's England, of Spenser's England, and the memory of her, and of her cottage by the brown, bright river, often comes back to me across the width of years. She was a perfectly well-bred person; she made one welcome to her little home with simple, perfect courtesy, without flutter, or fuss, or any effort of any sort; she had neither envy nor servility; grateful for all kindness, she never either abused the 'gentry' or flattered them; and her admirable manner never varied to the peddler at her door or to the squire of her village; would never have varied, I am sure, if the Queen of her country had crossed her doorstep. For she had the repose of contentment, of simplicity, and of that self-respect which can never exist where envy and effort are. She could neither read nor write; she scrubbed and washed and worked for herself; she had never left that one little green nook of Derbyshire, or seen other roads than the steep shady highway which went up to the pinewoods behind her house ; but she was a perfectly well-bred woman, born of a time calmer, broader, wiser, more generous than ours."

But Ouida's most mature work in criticism both of books and men is to be found in the *Critical Studies*. The literary articles contain her reasoned and permanent views of the literary art, and her criticism of French and Italian novelists is especially good. It is curious to note how in her criticism of the work of others she continually condemns the faults most prominent in her own. She was the first to bring the work of Gabriele d' Annunzio to the notice of the English public. She clearly saw both his weakness and his strength. Foreign influence, she declares, is not beneficial to the Italian. He can rarely steep his mind deeply in all the riches of foreign literature without losing some of his Italian individuality. D' Annunzio " allows himself to be absorbed and assimilated by foreign influences, to be dominated by them to so great an extent indeed that his style is frequently bastardized by them, and many of his sentences read as though they were translations from foreign sources. He claims to have greatly embellished and amplified the Italian language ; he has certainly rendered it more colloquial and more copious, but he has often grafted foreign idioms upon it, and he has perhaps robbed it of some of its dignity and grace. He considers that the artist should always remodel the instrument he uses ; but the figure will not hold good in other arts, for Sarasate does not carve the shell of his violin, Clausen does not weave the canvas he uses, Bartolomé does not blast the marble out of the hill-side. The writer should use the language he writes in as it comes pure from its natural springs, he will but contaminate it if he pour it into alien streams."

It is strange to find her complaining of the absolute absence in all D' Annunzio's works of wit, mirth, or humour, qualities conspicuously lacking in her own work. The melancholy spirit of his books she attributes to "that dull greyness of death which has spread from the laboratories of science over all the worlds of literature. Not only is no joyous laugh ever heard, there is not even the indulgent smile which relieves melancholy and bitterness in many writers whose views of life are gloomy." Ouida praises his women characters : " D' Annunzio draws women with exquisite veracity and skill, and a rare intuition into the workings of their minds and the beatings of their hearts. . . . They are wondrous presentments of breathing life. . . . He has incarnated the incomparable charm of the Italian woman, the most graceful, the most impassioned, the most seductive woman on earth, although also perhaps the most imperious, pitiless, and fiercely exacting in her passions." She notes his sympathy with the melody of birds, "the more singular in D'Annunzio because Italians are almost invariably indifferent to such melody, and snare the divine songster in the net, or shoot him whilst he shouts his nuptial *Io Triumphe!* with the most stolid indifference."

In an essay on Georges Darien, whose novels are filled with accusations against the conduct of France and the French during the Franco-German War, Ouida reveals her horror of war and her belief that authors should tell the truth at all costs, a difficult matter, so she considers, except in France. "Of all countries, France remains the land in which it is possible to tell the most truth. The nation of Montaigne and Molière is always the first to recognize and award the title of talent to lay bare the shoulders of her community and use the scourge upon them." She gives Darien's novels of the war the highest praise. "To represent war as it is done in the terrible pages of *La Débâcle*, or in the heartrending sketch of the *Attaque du Moulin*, is not difficult to the novelist who has power and knowledge. To represent the effects of war on entirely uninteresting and commonplace persons, and yet keep the attention of the reader riveted to what is passing in one ordinary household during a frightful national calamity, is a far more difficult feat." It is that feat which Darien accomplishes. "It seems to me," Ouida writes, "that in no contemporary fiction do we possess studies of spectacles, of sentiments, of street-life in a momentous hour, more accurate, more vivid, more simple in diction, more touching in suggestion."

In "Unwritten Literary Laws" we have Ouida's confession of literary faith. She declaims against the over-production of books which are not literature: "If this stream of pseudo-literature be not stopped, it will carry away and swamp all true English literature under it." She also points out the absurdity of insisting that a book must be of a certain length if it is to be successful with the British public. "The brevity or length of a literary work can have nothing to do with its beauty or excellence. If it be beautiful, if it be excellent, its proportions will be those which naturally grew out of its subject; and the writer who is an artist will know, as the painter knows, that he cannot alter the unwritten law which prescribes to him those proportions." She thinks there should be some means of legal protection against plagiarism, from which she considered herself to have greatly suffered, but that no one should sue another for any mere expression of opinion, however hostile or rudely expressed, "as Mr. Whistler sued Mr. Ruskin, for the liberty of the Press is of more importance than the annoyance of individuals." She objects to the anonymity of the Press. Every one ought to have the courage to sign his opinions.

Ouida devotes many articles to criticism of contemporary social conditions, and everywhere deplores the loss of beauty to which she attributes the evils of modern life. As early as 1881 she had written words in which we almost seem to hear Ruskin speaking :—

"Compare the mechanic of Wakefield or Blackburn, with the pall of black soot hung for ever between him and the sun, and his superficial repetitions of Darwin or Bradlaugh urged as evidence of an enlightened mind ; compare his automatic hideous toil, his hard hatred of all classes save his own, his dwelling one amidst rows of a thousand similar, his wilderness of dark, foul-scented streets, his stench of smoke, his talk of agnosticism and equality narrow as the routine of his life, his shallow sophisms, his club, his strikes, his tommy-shop ; compare him and these with the Italian labourer of the Luchese hills, or the Santa Fiora forests, or the Val d' Arno farms, rising to see the glorious sky glow like a summer rose, dwelling in his wide, stout, stone-built house old as the trees around him, following in their course as the seasons change his manly and healthful labours, reaping and binding, sowing and mowing, guiding his oxen through the vines, having for ever around him the gladdest and most gracious nature ; at noontide sitting down as the patriarch sat amidst his family and labourers to a homely plenty ; at eventide resting to see the youths and maidens dance, and listen to the old pastoral love songs sung to the thrum of the guitar or the story of the *Gerusalemme Liberata* passed down by word of mouth from sire to son." [1]

Later on, in dealing with what she called the ugliness of modern life, she compares present conditions with earlier ones, and sees little gain in so-called progress.

" Admit that the poorer people were ill-lodged in the Middle Ages, that the houses were ill-lit, undrained, with the gutter-water splashing the threshold, and the eaves of the opposite houses so near that the sun could not penetrate into the street. All this may have been so, but around two-thirds of the town were gardens and fields, the neighbouring streets were full of painted shrines, metal lamps, gargoyles, pinnacles, balconies of hand-forged iron or hand-carved stone, solid doors, bronzed gates, richly coloured frescoes ; and the eyes and hearts of the dwellers in them had wherewithal to feed on with pleasure, not to speak of the constant stream of many-coloured costume and of varied pageant procession which was for ever passing through them. Then in the niches there were figures ; at the corners there were shrines ; on the rivers there were beautiful carved bridges, of which examples are still left to our day in the Rialto and the Vecchio. There were barges with picture-illumined sails, and pleasure-galleys gay to the sight, and everywhere there were towers and spires, and

[1] *A Village Commune.*

crenellated walls, and the sculptured fronts of houses and churches and monasteries, and close at hand was the greenness of wood and meadow, the freshness of the unsullied country. Think only what that meant : no miles on miles of dreary suburban waste to travel ; no pert aggressive modern villas to make day hateful ; no underground railway-stations and subways ; no hissing steam, no grinding and shrieking cable-trams ; no hell of factory smoke and jerry-builders, lath and plaster ; no glaring geometrical flower-beds ; but the natural country running, like a happy child laden with posies, right up to the walls of the town.

" The cobbler or craftsman who sat and worked in his doorway, and saw the whole varicoloured life of a mediæval city pass by him, was a very different being to the modern mechanic, a cipher amongst hundreds, shut in a factory room amongst the deafening noise of cogwheels and pistons. Even from a practical view of his position, his guilds were a very much finer organization than modern trades-unions, and did far more for him in his body and his mind. In the exercise of his labour he could then be individual and original, he is now but one-thousandth part of an inch in a single tooth of a huge revolving cogwheel."

There is much truth here, but we cannot put the clock back, and if we could, it is doubtful if many of us would wish to do so.

Ouida's general attitude to politics is clear from her letters, but the passionate expression of her views reached its climax in the verses to Queen Victoria, and in the article on Joseph Chamberlain. Let us now examine the latter.

After observing that the Secretaryship of the Colonies was a somewhat subordinate post, though men of distinction like Lord Carnarvon and the first Lord Lytton had occupied it, Ouida admitted that no one ever made of the department the throne of the Suprema Lex, as Mr. Chamberlain did. She then proceeds to discover the reason of this ; as she puts it, "the fault of whom, or the fault of what, lies at the root of this successful usurpation."

"In an epoch more courageous, more honest, more well-bred than the present, a great party calling itself Conservative would have repulsed with contempt any renegade Radical, however disguised in the domino of a Unionist. Instead, this party has received him with open arms, nay, with prostrate self-effacement, and worshipped him with enthusiasm ; indeed, the victory of the so-called Tories at the urns in 1895 would not have been possible if Chamberlain had not permitted it ; which he would not have done unless he had been assured that he would enter and dominate the Salisbury Cabinet. He has been equally happy in the occasions which have presented themselves to him, and in his own capability in using them ; in the mediocrity of the men who combine with him, and of the men who oppose him ; in his infinite ability in influencing the first, and in intimidating the last ; he

has been fortunate also in the fact that the English
people are less bigoted in religion than of old ; for
in an earlier time they would have seen with horror
a Unitarian entering the Government. But his greatest
good fortune of all was in the rise of the Home Rule
Question at the very moment when he conceived the
project of going over to the Tory camp, which,
without such an opportune reason to give for it, would
have appeared mere unworthy treachery. Without the
platform of Home Rule from which to make his *saut
périlleux*, the leap would have probably broken his
neck ; at any rate he could not have made it with
the certainty of being welcomed and rewarded by his
new allies, and of occupying amongst them a position
far more conspicuous than he ever occupied with the
Radicals."

Ouida held Chamberlain responsible for "the
financiers' war in South Africa" as she termed it.
"He might have called it proudly ' *My war*,' as the
Empress Eugénie called the war with Germany ' *Ma
guerre à moi.*' If he had never been anything higher
than Mayor of Birmingham, the farmers of the
Transvaal would still be ploughing their lands in
peace."

She traces the phenomenon of Chamberlain wielding
such great power over Cabinet and country to the
lingering influence of Disraeli :—

"Disraeli and his influence have dominated and
penetrated English political and social atmospheres,

Ouida : a Memoir

in their highest strata, as a contagious fever enters and reigns in a district. It was a strange phenomenon, the Venetian Jew leading by the leash the entire English aristocracies. To trace the manifold reasons which enabled a man so alien and antipathetic to the British nation in blood, in manner, in appearance, in opinions, to dominate that nation so completely would require many folio volumes ; for there has never been anything more singular, or more due to innumerable causes, all converging to one end.

"No spectacle is more extraordinary than the power which Disraeli acquired after being laughed down by every one ; acquired and wields still, so many years after his death. I think that his most potent philtre lay in his flattery. He flattered his Sovereign, his party, and the nation itself, with all the florid eloquence and subtle suggestion of which he was so admirable a master. His famous ' Peace with Honour ' was an exact sample of his style ; the peace was brittle and the honour was dubious, but his manner of presenting them was so magnificent that they were received as though they were gifts from heaven. . . .

" . . . The first step taken, the rest followed ; the mania of what is considered aggrandisement has acquired possession of the national life, and has made of a nation, naturally noble and great, a swollen boaster, bawling of its millions, its might, and its superiority, although surely vanity is no more admirable in a country than in an individual."

Ouida as Critic

Chamberlain continued Disraeli's work, but by vulgarizing and brutalizing it.

The article ends with some general criticism of the Victorian age.

"The reign of Queen Victoria has been a long succession of wars; few, if any, were either necessary or inevitable. But not one of these has been a war of defence at home; the English citizen and peasant know nothing in their own land of the horrors of war; they have never seen its desolation and its horrors; they have never seen their little children crushed under the hoofs and wheels of a battery, their homes set on fire by a shell, their sons starving, their fields devastated, their towns beleaguered. They have never seen a battle, a siege, a trench full of dead; therefore they do not know the hideous suffering which they inflict when they let loose, in pride of spirit and lightness of heart and triumphant vanity, the fiends of war upon a distant people and a far-off land. This is the excuse of a large portion of the nation for the present war; but it is at the same time the strongest condemnation of those who preach war to it as a divine creed, and appeal to its most brutal instincts, and abuse its ignorance to lead it into crime. The victories now gained will be dearly bought, for they, and the national madness they produce, will certainly set Joseph Chamberlain in the seat of supreme power, and no one will have the courage to restrain his hand. Bellona has served him so well now, she will be his chosen handmaid in the future."

Between Ouida's opinions and her way of life there was slight accord. While herself adopting the surroundings and ways of living of the rich, and infinitely preferring their society, provided they were also persons of rank, she constantly attacked them. She declared among other things that the rich can never suffer physical pain as the poor do. Admitting that a rich man has means to mitigate his sufferings in cases of illness—indeed, I have heard rich people say that therein lies the sole advantage of wealth—a stomach-ache must still cause as much pain to a rich man as to a poor one. Neither did Ouida believe that the rich often suffer much from what she calls " sorrows of the soul," and for the reason that the rich man is usually a complete egotist, whose philanthropy has a political purpose or a social ambition as its mainspring. But a poor man can be as great an egotist as a rich one. She ignored the fact that money can be a very beautiful thing in the hands of those who know how to use it, and that many generous impulses die for lack of the money to carry them through. Yet in spite of their vehemence, of their partiality, and of some exaggeration, these critical essays are worth careful study by a generation which in its pride in its swiftly advancing progress seldom takes time to pause and look back.

IX

OUIDA AS
HUMANITARIAN
AND SOCIAL
REFORMER

CHAPTER IX

OUIDA AS HUMANITARIAN AND SOCIAL REFORMER

OUIDA'S sympathy with the suffering and oppressed, whether human beings or dumb
animals, is amply evident in her writings and actions.

Everywhere in her writings she expresses her
horror of war, but her feeling in that matter is well
summed up in an article in the *Fortnightly Review*
entitled, "Watchman, What of the Night?" [1] She
deals there with the serious import to European
nations of Japan's victory over Russia, and with the
folly of war in general.

"The immeasurable physical suffering, mental
torture, bereavement, destruction, and incalculable
ruin caused by war are ignored and not weighed
for a moment. It needs no professional knowledge
to perceive that each successive war is more murderous
and on a vaster scale than its immediate predecessor.
Every year sees the engines of slaughter increased
in numbers and in power. The youthful and able-
bodied are swept away to each campaign in greater

[1] May, 1905.

301

numbers than in the preceding one, and the aged, the maimed, the sickly are left in their homes with the womenkind. To what can this tend? It would be comic, if it were not tragic, to see the boastful vaunts of the scientists of all they do for the ameliora-tion of human life, whilst, side by side with their medical schools and laboratories, there stand the cannon-foundries, the powder-magazines, the factories of explosives, the docks containing the torpedoes, the submarines, and all the other manufactories for whole-sale human destruction."

Ouida considered that military despotism had increased throughout Europe since the Franco-German War of 1870–71. Such despotism, she declared, brought with it "the impoverishment of the people, the curse of youth and man-hood, the endless strain of a fiscal burden so enor-mous that every class groans under it, and the perpetual and diseased anxiety in which every nation lives, suspecting its neighbours, and turn by turn affronting them insolently and cringing to them obsequiously, according as it is made to feel the power of its own strength or the weakness of its own inferiority." [1]

She equally disapproved of war where conscription was not the rule, as may be learnt from her strictures on the Boer War in both her public and private utterances.

She was a foe to oppressive taxation of the poor,

[1] Cf. *Critical Studies*, "Georges Darien."

and, as we have seen, many of her novels, the scenes of which are laid in Italy, deal with the effects of the oppressive taxation of the people by the Italian monarchical government. She exaggerated the sins of the ruling and official classes, but there is much truth in her statements. The Italian is, she declares, governed to death, "and tied up in the stifling network of an infinity of small ordinances and wearisome prohibitions. . . . The rural communes of the country have more than a milliard of debts, almost all due to the senseless mania for demolition, for novelty, for superfluous alterations and imitations, works worse than useless, commended or proposed by the Government, and eagerly accepted by the communal and provincial councils, since each member of these hoped to rub his share of gilding off the gingerbread as it passed through his hands. All the vast sums thus expended are taken out of the enormous local and imperial taxation, are divided between contractors, engineers, members of the town and county councils, lawyers, go-betweens, and all the innumerable middlemen who swarm in every community like mites in cheese, at the same time that the poor peasant is taxed at the gates for a half-dozen of eggs or a bundle of grass, and the poor washerwoman carrying in her linen has her petticoats pulled up over her head by a searcher to ascertain if she have nothing saleable or taxable hidden on her person." [1]

[1] Cf. *Critical Studies*, "The Decadence of Latin Races."

Ouida : a Memoir

Ouida's vehement defence of the poor Italian peasant was born of a sincere desire to help him, and she expended both time and money in her efforts to ameliorate his lot.

But it is, above all, Ouida's efforts for the amelioration of the conditions under which dumb animals, especially dogs, birds, and horses, live in civilized communities that mark her out as a worker in the humanitarian cause.

"'God made men and women.'

"'Yes. But I wonder if the trapped birds, and the beaten dogs, and the smarting mules, and the bleeding sheep think so.'

"'O, Signa !'

"'I think they must doubt it,' said Signa.

"'But the beasts are not Christians, the priests say so,' said Palma, who was a very true believer.

"'I know. But I think they are. They forgive— we never do.'" [1]

These words illustrate Ouida's attitude towards the whole of the dumb creation.

The earliest reference of importance in her writings that testifies to her feeling for animals occurs in *Puck*,[2] where she puts the following observations into the mouth of the dog who relates the story :—

"You think you have no slaves in England ! Why, half the races in creation moan, and strive, and suffer,

[1] *Signa.*   [2] 1871.

304

daily and hourly, under your merciless tyrannies ! No slaves ! Ask the ox, with his bloodshot, agonized eyes, mutilated for the drover's gain ere he is driven to his end in the slaughter-house. Ask the sheep, with their timid, woe-begone faces, scourged into the place of their doom, bruised and bleeding and tortured. Ask the racer, spent ere he reaches his prime by unnatural strains on strength and speed, that he may fill the pockets of your biggest blackguards with misbegotten gold ; old whilst yet he is young, poisoned in the hours of his victory, caressed by princes in the moment that he ministers to their greed, cast off to street hire and hourly misery in the worthless years of his weary age. Ask the cart-horse, doomed through a long life of labour to strive and stagger under burdens, to bear heat and cold, and hunger and stripes, without resistance ; fed grudgingly, paid for willing toil by merciless blows, killed by doing the work of men as the Egyptian slave died in the lifting of the last stone to the King's Temple, or consigned, as the only recompense for years of usefulness and patience, to the brutalities of the dissecting-room or the knacker's yard. Ask *us* !

"What ! You tell me this is but the issue of an inevitable law ? Ay, so it is ; of the law of the stronger over the weaker. But whilst you thus follow out that law on millions of chained and beaten and tortured creatures, have conscience enough, I pray you, not to brag aloud that you keep no slaves, not to bawl from the housetops of your reverence for freedom.

" When will you give a Ten Hours Bill for horses—a Prohibitive Act against the racing of one- or two-year-olds ?—a Protection Order for Cattle ?—and an Emancipation Movement for chained dogs ? Nay, when will you do so much as remember that the coward who tortures an animal would murder a human being if he were not afraid of the gallows ? When will you see that to teach the hand of a child to stretch out and smother the butterfly is to teach that hand, when a man's, to steal out and strangle an enemy ? "

A little later Puck, in describing a young girl, observes in phrases that are reminiscent of Shelley's " Sensitive Plant " :—

" Now and then, too, she moved aside, that her foot should not crush some tiny crawling thing, that had its one short hour of harmless joy amongst the leaves and grasses : now and then she lifted some little brown glow-worm, with its brightly burning lamp, up to some place of safety, on a leafy bough, or in the cup of a late lily : nay, even a beetle creeping with its load home-ward, or even a sand-worm crawling on the gravelled way, she stepped aside from, leaving them their life.

" Would that more amongst you had that tender pity, had that reverence for the wonder of existence

which is as great in the tiniest fly that wings its
way as in the great leviathan of the sea. All things
must suffer and must think, since all things dread
and trust : can there be fear without mental torture?
Can there be trust without emotional power ? Ay
—and thrusting a pin through the beetle's body and
cutting the brain from a living pigeon, in your
hideous dissecting-rooms, will not teach you this ; it
will only teach you to be blind to it."

Ouida constantly inculcated kindness to animals on
children of her acquaintance. A little boy [1] wrote to
her in 1892 for her autograph. She sent it, accompanied by her volume of stories *Bimbi*, a book
that amply testifies to Ouida's extraordinarily
strong affection for dogs. He acknowledged it,
and two months later (March 10, 1893) received
this letter :—

"MY DEAR STEWART,—

"Enrol yourself in this Guild and I will send
you another book at Christmas.

"Ever yours,

"OUIDA."

Enclosed was a prospectus of the Guild of Gentleness, a society for promoting kindness to birds and
animals among young people, set on foot by the
Manchester Weekly Times.

[1] Stewart M. Ellis.

Ouida : a Memoir

To another little boy [1] Ouida wrote :—

"MY DEAR BERTIE,—

". . . Don't think I do not like you because
I want to see you gentler to animals. You are a
bright and clever boy, and ought to understand that
animals being so entirely in our power, all unkind
use of our strength over them is both mean and
unworthy. Try and remember that. Real manli-
ness is always indulgent and never tyrannical. Perhaps long after I am dead you will show this to
your children and say, This is what I was told by—
                                        "OUIDA."

Willie Strange, a small boy, son of Alderman
Strange, of Eastbourne, was fined by the magistrates
for allowing a pet dog to be at large unmuzzled.
The case was reported, and soon after the youthful
defendant received from Italy the following letter :—

                    "*January* 24th [? 1907].
"MY DEAR BOY,—

"I have seen your action, as recorded in the
papers, with much pleasure. Any devotion you pay
to your dog will be repaid to you a thousandfold by
his affection. 'Tis only men who betray those who
befriend them. The muzzling craze is a brutal folly
and a disgrace to England.

[1] H. Danyell-Tassinari.

308

Ouida as Humanitarian

"Accept this little half-napoleon for your savings-box, and if ever I can be useful to you or your dog, command me.

"I remain,
"Yours with much sympathy,
"OUIDA."

Any one who loved dogs easily won Ouida's heart. In a letter to Captain Danyell she says :—

"G. W.[1] wrote me when he was Governor of Cyprus that he loved dogs as much as I could do, and that wherever he commanded no dog should ever be hurt or tormented! How many great men have loved Dogs! I think it is the frank, free, fond faith of the creature which is so welcome a contrast to them with the world of flatterers and of foes !"

She took part in resisting the Dog Act of 1870, a resistance that was supported by Bulwer Lytton. She constantly wrote in the public Press on behalf of dogs.[2] She declared that if people who kept dogs would learn a little more about them they would not think that so many dogs had hydrophobia. "I believe that the much-talked-of rabies would never be known if dogs were rationally treated and free to be happy in their own natural way."

---

[1] Garnet Wolseley.
[2] Cf., e.g., "A Plea on Behalf of Dogs," first printed (1878) in the *Whitehall Review*, and reprinted in *The Animal World* (May, 1878) ; *A Treatise on Dogs*, 1897.

But few persons take the trouble to study their pets morally and physically.

" The study of my four-footed companions has so persuaded me of their singular intelligence, their acute sensibility, and their most generous temper ; their playful ways have diverted for me so many an idle or tedious hour ; and their loyalty, their truthfulness, and their good faith have so often consoled me for the rarity of these qualities in human nature, that I do but pay back a debt I owe when I endeavour, by any words that it is in my power to use, to plead for a little justice in this world to my dear comrades—the Dogs."

Ouida has much to say on the right feeding of dogs. She sets out a dietary : their tastes must be consulted, the food freshly cooked and plentiful. People cannot expect, she declares, " to keep a dog for nothing," They should have boiled liver and bread at 11 a.m., beef and rice at 7 p.m. Big dogs may have captain biscuits, little dogs sponge cakes ; bones may be given them to amuse them, but must never be regarded as a substitute for food. It is a fallacy to think that rich foods hurt them. In telling us that she gave her own dogs everything they chose that she herself had—rich soups, game, sweet cakes, salmis, timbales, petits pâtés—she incidentally lets in light on her housekeeping.

She habitually watched the animals about her, whether her pets or the natural inhabitants of her garden, and whatever she notes as the result of her observations is full of interest. Those observations are doubtless tinged with some of the imagination that came so readily to her call, but she studied the ways and habits of horses, dogs, and birds with loving care. Here are some notes on her horses, with the general conclusions drawn from them :—

"I am, at the present moment, driving a mare who was always driven with her sister, who died eighteen months ago. She does not forget her sister, and the stable companion given her instead she hates, and endeavours, with all her might, to kick and bite across the pole and in the stalls. I owned also a pony so attached to his comrade that they could live in the same loose-box together, and when the companion died, this pony was miserable, whinnied and neighed perpetually, lost health, and in a few months died also. In life he was the humble and devoted slave of his brother, would fondle him, clean him, follow him about in all directions, and show to him every testimony of affection possible in one creature to another. Yet such feelings as these, although very common in animals, are never remembered or considered for an instant, and animals of all kinds are sold from owner to owner, and hustled from place to place, with no more regard than if they were chairs and tables. What they suffer from strange voices, new homes,

and unfamiliar treatment no one inquires, for no
one cares. Convenience and profit are all which are
considered. There is little or no remembrance of
the idiosyncrasy of each creature. The ecstatic,
ardent, nervous temperament of the dog ; the timid,
imaginative, impulsive mind of the horse ; the shrink-
ing shyness of the sheep, the attachment to place and
people of the wildest or silliest creature when once
kindly treated and long domesticated—all these things
are never recollected or considered in dealing with
them." [1]   Here are two notes on the ways of birds :—

"As I write this a robin hops up the stone balus-
trade of the terrace ; he looks at me brightly and
fearlessly. There is a large bamboo in a pottery
vase on the top of the terrace ; he hops up to it
and busies himself inside its branches for awhile,
then looks at me again, flies away on to another
bamboo which grows on the lawn, and sings a song
of thanks. How lovely are all his movements ;
how beautiful is his glance ; how bright is the sheen
of his plumage ; how charming are his buoyancy
and confidence ! Kill him ! As soon would I kill a
child that loved me." [2]

She always declared that when birds were supposed
to be destroying fruit, they were really eating insects
invisible to us.

[1] Cf. *Views and Opinions* (1895), "Death and Pity."
[2] Cf. "Birds and their Persecutors" in *Toxin and Other Papers*,
1896 (Tauchnitz).

Ouida as Humanitarian

" I saw a blackbird one day occupied at a bunch of ripe grapes on my wall. Poised on outstretched wings, he kept incessantly darting at it, and continued to do so for many minutes. When he at last flew away I went and looked at the bunch : he had not perforated or touched a single grape ; therefore he had of course been eating the insects and aphidæ within the cluster." [1]

Ouida considered that not only is the affection of animals undervalued by man, but that man greatly underrates their intelligence.

" Man having but one conception of intelligence, his own, does not endeavour to comprehend another which is different, and differently exhibited and expressed. . . . If our mind exceeds the mind of animals and birds in much, theirs exceeds ours at least in some things, as their sight, scent, and hearing far surpass ours.

" When we remember also that these other races are absolutely alone, are never aided by man, are only, on the contrary, hindered by him, opposed, thwarted, and persecuted by him, their achievements are, relatively to their opportunities, much more wonderful than any of his. The elements which are his great foes are likewise theirs ; they have to encounter and suffer all the woes of tempest, hurricane, flood, the width of barren seas, the

[1] Cf. " Birds and their Persecutors " in *Toxin and Other Papers*, 1896 (Tauchnitz).

hunger on solitary shores; and they have also in his
ruthless and unceasing spite an enemy more cruel
than any with which he himself has to contend.
If we meditate on this unquestionable fact, we shall
be forced to admit that Cristoforo Colombo was
not a greater hero than many a little swallow. . . .

"There is no sympathy with these interesting and
mysterious lives led side by side with man, but
ignored by him entirely, except when by him
persecuted. The nest of the weaver-bird is to the
full as ingenious and as marvellous as the dome of
St. Peter's or St. Paul's. The beaver State and the
bee State are as intricate in organization as the
Constitution of the French Republic and the British
Monarchy, and are distinctly superior in many parts
of their organization to either of these. The passage
of the white ants through a jungle and across a
continent is quite as admirable in unison and skill
and order as the human march to Chitral; and the
annual flights of the storks, of the Solan geese, of
the wild ducks, exhibit qualities of obedience to a
chosen commander, of endurance, of observation,
and of wisdom, not exceeded by any human Arctic
or Australian exploring party."[1]

Ouida's efforts against any sort of cruelty practised
on animals were untiring. She took some share in
starting the Italian Society for the Prevention of
Cruelty to Animals, and was indefatigable in bringing

[1] Cf. *Critical Studies*, "The Quality of Mercy."

cases to its notice. She wrote many articles against the destruction of birds and trees in Italy. She ascribed the cruelty of earlier times to violence, that of modern times to cowardice and selfishness. She often complains in letters to her friends of the increasing hardness and brutality of men as regards animals. Motoring seemed to her one of the factors in that attitude. She wrote to Mr. Henry S. Salt, Honorary Secretary of the Humanitarian League, a society in which she took much interest and whose aims she helped with her pen, in 1901 : " Motoring, too, is surely a hardening and brutalizing factor, and I do not think that the keen motorist feels any pang at the deaths he causes : why did the stupid creature get in the way? Human life seems to me much coarser and ruder than it was even twenty-five years ago."

She allowed scarcely anything connected with cruelty to animals to pass without making a protest of some kind. On the occasion of the " Distance Ride " from Berlin to Vienna and back in 1895 by German officers, she wrote the following letter, entitled " Decorated Butchers," to Dr. William Evans Darby, Secretary of the Peace Society :—

" Any one who has forced himself to read the sickening details of the ' Distance Ride ' from Berlin to Vienna, and *vice versâ*, must be struck by the frightful injury to the moral feeling of the populace of both nations done by this horrible spectacle of legalized and honoured torture. It is absolutely useless for laws to be framed, and societies to be formed for the prevention of cruelty and the inculcation of humanity, when Sovereigns, Princes and 'Gentlemen' lend themselves to commit and to admire such brutality. If the riders had desired to prove their own endurance, they could have done so equally well with relays of horses; and the disgusting agony inflicted on the noble beasts which they have tortured and murdered would not have been given, in all its demoralizing infamy, to the public. To summon and fine, or imprison, a carter, for overworking his horse, whilst an *officer* who has ridden his charger to death is feasted and decorated by Emperors is one of those examples of 'one measure for the rich and another for the poor' which are the justification of the Anarchist. Every one of these decorated butchers who have been received and applauded by the young Kaiser and the old one, at Berlin and Vienna, should be degraded and imprisoned, if there be any reality whatever in the laws against cruelty and in the professions of civilization. It is wholly useless to preach mercy to the multitudes, when, along the highways, they can behold men of royal and noble blood spurring their animals to death, or dragging them into the goal 'dripping with blood, sweating and screaming with agony, the spines twisted out of shape, the hoofs dropping off from inflammation.'"

The wanton destruction of birds in Italy greatly

exercised her mind. When in 1902 the late Mr. E. B.
Caulfield, then editor of the *Italian Gazette*, asked
Ouida for a contribution, she replied : " You ask me
for some words to inaugurate your editorship of the
English Florentine paper : how can I better comply
with your request than by asking you and your
subscribers and readers to do all they can to protect
the birds of Tuscany ? " [1] The article is an eloquent
plea for bird life. Here is one passage :—

" Would that any words of mine could make the
villa gardens, and the green woods of plain and hill
and riverside around Florence sanctuaries for these
fair creatures, whether natives of the soil or pilgrims
from afar, whether coming weary and exhausted over
deserts and seas, or nesting in leafy nooks wherever
their ancestors were allowed to be at peace. Nothing
is more touching than to watch swallows and martins
returning with unerring accuracy to the grey timbers
or the brown tiles where season after season they and
theirs have reared their callow broods ; nothing is more
lovely than to hear the nesting song of the nightingale
rising in the moonlight from the laurel-shaded grasses,
or the roots of the fragrant bay-tree where, with the
winds and the dews of April, year after year he sings
his epithalamium."

Over and over again she pointed out how the woods

[1] The article is reprinted in the *Italian Gazette* for January 28,
1913. Discussion on Bird Protection was being carried on in some
of the Italian newspapers.

made by nature a paradise for birds had become silent and uninhabited. The Italian, she averred, classed them as vermin and failed to appreciate the " exquisite loveliness of movement, of form, of mode of life, which makes even a songless bird a miracle of charm and poetry." Birds in Italy were hunted from dawn to dark, and meanwhile insect plagues increased, because the larvæ-eating and the insect-killing birds were murdered in the very season of their usefulness. "Who lets the swallows, who would rid the air of winged pests in their graceful circling flight, be shot down in scores as they flash in the morning sun or skim the water at even-time for a bath and drink ? I have known hundreds of swallows and martins come to make their nests as April brought them home, and I have known these innocent and useful returning pilgrims destroyed almost entirely before June was passed, two or three at most being left of the happy bands which had come back so joyously and trustingly to the roofs of men. All day long this bird in its buoyant flight is ridding the air of men's worst pests." How, then, can man bring himself to destroy a creature of such beauty, grace, and fidelity, with his ingenuity in architecture, his intelligence in travel and self-guidance ?

The life of a bird, she writes, " is such a lovely little life—cradled amongst the hawthorn buds, searching for aphidæ amongst apple blossoms, drinking dew from the cup of a lily ; awake when the grey light breaks in the east, throned on the topmost branch of a tree, swinging with it in the sunshine, flying from it through the air ; then the friendly quarrel with a neighbour over a worm or berry ; the joy of bearing grass seed to his mate where she sits down amongst the docks and daisies ; the triumph of singing the praise of sunshine or of moonlight ; the merry, busy, useful days ; the peaceful sleep, steeped in the scent of the closed flowers, with head under one wing and the leaves forming a green roof above."

Ouida disliked the idea of shutting up any animals in cages, and when Mr. Salt asked her to write an article on the iniquity of feeding the reptiles at the Zoological Gardens with live animals, she replied :—

[VIAREGGIO]
"*May* 23 [1907].

" I cannot write an article on the snake feeding, for I have hurt one of my eyes and must use both as little as possible. But it is infamous, inconceivably so. . . . No object is gained by the public spectacle of this horror, and its impression on tender-hearted children must be exceedingly painful and do much harm. . . . I abhor all Zoological Gardens, and they are certainly very bad for children."

She foresaw a time when animals and birds would disappear from off the face of the earth.

" The great beauty which animal and bird life lends

to the earth is doomed to lessen and disappear. The automatic vehicle will render the horse useless ; and he will be considered too costly, and too slow, to be kept even as a gambling toy. The dog will have no place in a world which has no gratitude for such simple sincerity and faithful friendliness as he offers. When wool, and horn, and leather, and meat foods have been replaced by chemical inventions, cattle and sheep will have no more tolerance than the wild buffalo has had in the United States. What are now classed as big game will be exterminated in Asia and Africa, and already in Europe we are told that the pleasure it affords to people to kill them is the sole reason why stags, foxes, and game-birds are allowed to exist and multiply under artificial protection. All the charm which the races of 'fur and feather' lend to the earth will be lost for ever ; for a type destroyed can never be recalled."

Ouida loved trees and flowers almost as much as she loved animals, and regarded with sorrow and misgiving the destruction of trees that went on in Italy.

"There is a modern custom in Italy, which is typical of the havoc made by avarice and indifference and commerce running together hand in hand. It is the shocking habit of stripping all evergreen trees of their leaves to sell them to chemists, gilders, dyers, and the managers of what in France we call *pompes funèbres*. Even magnolias are not spared. . . . The injury done to the trees is, of course, immeasurable. After a few seasons they become anæmic, dry up, and slowly perish, whilst the aspect of the gardens of which the bay, myrtle, box, laurel, arbutus, and magnolia were of late such conspicuous ornaments is, of course, utterly changed and ruined."

She also protested wherever and whenever she could against the wanton rooting up of wild flowers, especially in the woods and meadows round Florence.

Sport, at least all kinds of it that involved the taking of animal life, was abhorrent to her and came in for castigation. "When men kill in self-defence it is natural ; when they kill for food it is excusable ; but to kill for pleasure and for paltry pride is vile. How long will such pleasure and such pride be the rule of the world ? They give the strongest justification that Anarchists can claim." [1] The practice of game-preserving, of hunting the hare, fox, or stag, of big-game shooting is always severely dealt with : "The gun is the weapon of the gentleman, as in other days was the rapier or the sword ; the gun-room is his *Academe*." She deplores that sport has become fashionable even with women, for sport, in Ouida's view, inevitably creates deadness of feeling, and no one could take pleasure in it who was sensitive to suffering.[2] "I am certain," she wrote to Mr. Salt, "that sport as seen in this day in its effect on character produces a sort of insanity, a kind of delirium akin to drunkenness." In private letters and in the public Press she

[1] Cf. *Views and Opinions*, "Death and Pity."
[2] Cf. *Critical Studies*, "The Quality of Mercy."

gave vent to her indignation against the Eton College beagles. She declared that it was "a grotesque yet terrible thing that the nobility and gentry, the pastors and masters, of such a country as England should publicly uphold an amusement for youth which consists in the torture and mutilation of one of the most timid and innocent of animals," and even went so far as to address a strong letter of protest to the Headmaster.

She is especially severe on pigeon shooting from traps, which "unhappily English example has made popular and fashionable throughout Europe. Not a word can be said in its favour or defence. It is mean, cowardly, barbarous, and contemptible. A blue rock is a clever and handsome creature. I kept some once in a large enclosure to paint from, and was struck as I watched them by their brightness, vivacity, and intelligent communication with each other ; the dancing and the posturing of the males in courtship are delightfully droll. I have seen a male pigeon waltz round and round many times, raising his crest and flapping his wings, and then advance to his lady-love with mincing graces in a slow gavotte, bowing low at intervals, whilst she made believe not even to see him. And these interesting creatures are thrown pell-mell into hampers and sacks, with broken legs and wing feathers torn out, and after long racking journeys, half suffocated and tortured by thirst, become the targets for the crack shots of an aristocratic Society ! "

In early years, however, Ouida was not of this

opinion, for she records how the one act of her life for which she felt the most acute regret and remorse was that she once gave a silver cigar-case to be shot for at Hurlingham by the Lords and Commons. "My excuse, if it can be called one, is that *I did not think. . . .* It is an act of which I am now poignantly ashamed. When, later on, a wounded bird fluttered down to die beneath a cedar-tree by which I was seated, I realized the full horror of that disgusting sport, and I never again entered the enclosure of the club."

Ouida was, of course, an impassioned anti-vivisectionist. She never lost an opportunity of declaring her views, but her arguments may best be seen in an article entitled "The New Priesthood," [1] where they are stated with great violence.

She defends herself against any sentiment in the matter. "Every noble movement of the world has been saddled with this name, from patriotism to the abolition of slavery ; and every impersonal impulse of the human race is necessarily one of sentiment— *i.e.*, of spiritual and generous, as opposed to gross and merely egotistic, inspirations." Her great fear was that the practice would be continued from animals to human beings. "*There is not a single argument used by the advocates of vivisection which will not apply in as complete an entity to human, as to animal subjects.*" The italics are Ouida's.

She feared that vivisection would lead to the

[1] Cf. *Toxin and Other Papers* (Tauchnitz, 1896).

" scientific torture of lunatics,"[1] and protested against the use of lunatics for experiments in physiology or surgery. She declared that it was becoming a common practice, and was " the inevitable consequence of the heartless indifference of the world in general to the scientific torture of animals."

This is not the place to refute Ouida's arguments. They are mentioned here to illustrate her love of the dumb creation. But we cannot refrain from deploring her attitude throughout her work, both in her novels and in her essays, towards men of science in general and the medical and surgical profession in particular. When she dilates on the brutality of the surgeon, it becomes quite clear that she had never in her own person had experience of the kindness, the gentleness, the consideration, in a word the humanity, of a great and skilful surgeon. And even the most impartial mind could have scant patience with such a passage as the following :—

" If there be one thing more loathsome than the carnage of war, it is the Red Cross societies following in its train. But the modern world, being conscious that the butchery of war ill accords with its æsthetic and religious pretensions, gives a sop to its conscience by sending the ambulance side by side with the gun-carriage. A more robust and more honest temper did not evade the truth that the least brutal war is the one most immediately and conclusively destructive ; the

[1] Cf. *Humanity*, November, 1897.

slaughter of wounded men was more truly merciful than the modern system of surgery and nursing, which saves shattered constitutions and ruined health to drag out a miserable and artificially prolonged existence ! "

In a remarkable article contributed to *The Humane Review*,[1] entitled " The Culture of Cowardice," Ouida protests against " the concentration of the general mind on the prevention of disease." She deplores the " new hygiene" which teaches men and women " to see possible or probable death in everything which approaches them." Indeed—

" They are taught perpetually to endeavour to defend themselves from the proximity of death by the most minute cares and the most elaborate precautions ; they are to pass their whole existence in a stench of disinfectants ; they are to see deadly organisms in everything they touch ; they are to suspect injury to themselves in every breeze which blows ; they are to shrink in fear of contamination from the rosy lips of a little child, and flee from the good-natured gambols of a merry dog ; the pleasant odour of a freshly turned furrow to them speaks of poisonous exhalations and mephitic vapours ; the prick of a pin may mean tetanus, and the humming of a blue-bottle fly can only preface an inoculation of carbon."

Ouida argues curiously enough that disease has its

[1] July, 1900.

value, and is not nearly so terrible a scourge as war. It is, she declares, extremely illogical to bewail the death of five thousand persons by a visitation of typhoid or smallpox and to applaud the death of ten thousand persons in battle or in siege. War, too, kills men, not women, and millions of useful animals ; it kills in youth, rarely in age, in health, rarely in infirmity ; for one whom it kills outright it maims and invalidates ten, leaving them for the rest of their lives incomplete and suffering. She continues—

"Disease, on the contrary, kills more women than men, and therefore serves the world better ; kills outright one and allows hundreds to recover none the worse for the attack. It is much more merciful than war is, more discriminating also, for it usually only takes those who are predisposed to receive it. The convalescence which follows on disease may be a period of peace and gratitude, bringing with it a certain sweetness ; the recovery after wounds of shell, bullet, lance, or sabre is most irritating suffering, leaving long injury behind it."

The flaws in the argument are easily perceived, but it serves to show an original point of view and to what lengths Ouida's prejudices against the march of modern science, and especially against vivisection, led her. But she is not, perhaps, altogether wrong in protesting against and pointing out the evils of the over-preoccupation with hygiene that prevails to-day.

Ouida had the fixed idea that commerce, militarism,

and socialism were ruining all modern life, depriving it of the heights and depths, the lights and shades, that make the charm of life as of landscape. "When all the arable earth is one huge allotment-ground, a Corot will find no subject for his canvas, not even in his dreams, for his dreams will be dead of inanition." She even foresees a time when "the earth, having been all built over with brick, and the skies blackened with furnaces, and the lands all over peopled to the very edge of the farthest shores, the wretched crowds will look at landscape paintings in the public galleries and will say, 'Was ever the world like that? Was there ever space to breathe, and green leaves?'"

Mr. Wilfrid Scawen Blunt's estimate of Ouida's public work in the cause of humanity, written on purpose for this memoir, forms a fitting conclusion to this chapter :—

"As a public letter-writer and pamphleteer, few women have been ever more effective than Ouida. She had a courage and a command of whirling passionate words which forced themselves on public attention. Her exaggerated enthusiasms made readers smile, but they also made them think. It would be difficult to overstate the effect of her pleading for the weak things of the world, especially of the animal world, whose cause she made her own."

BIBLIOGRAPHY

Held in Bondage. 3 vols. (Tinsley.) 1863.

Strathmore. 3 vols. (Chapman and Hall.) 1865.

Chandos. 3 vols. (Chapman and Hall.) 1866.

Cecil Castlemaine's Gage and Other Novelettes. Collected and revised by the Author. (Chapman and Hall.) 1867.

Under Two Flags. 3 vols. (Chapman and Hall.) 1867.

Idalia. 3 vols. (Chapman and Hall.) 1867.

Tricotrin.[1] 2 vols. (Chapman and Hall.) 1869.

Puck. 3 vols. (Chapman and Hall.) 1870.

Folle-Farine. 3 vols. (Chapman and Hall.) 1871.

A Dog of Flanders and Other Stories. (Chapman and Hall.) 1872.

Pascarèl.[2] 3 vols. (Chapman and Hall.) 1873.

Two Little Wooden Shoes. (Chapman and Hall.) 1874.

Signa. 3 vols. (Chapman and Hall.) 1875.

In a Winter City. (Chapman and Hall.) 1876.

Ariadne. 3 vols. (Chapman and Hall and Chatto and Windus.) 1877.

Friendship. 3 vols. (Chatto and Windus.) 1878.

Moths. 3 vols. (Chatto and Windus.) 1880.

Pipistrello and Other Stories. (Chatto and Windus.) 1880.

A Village Commune.[3] 2 vols. (Chatto and Windus.) 1881.

Bimbi : Stories for Children.[4] (Chatto and Windus.) 1882.

In Maremma. 3 vols. (Chatto and Windus.) 1882.

Wanda. 3 vols. (Chatto and Windus.) 1883.

Frescoes : Dramatic Sketches.[5] (Chatto and Windus.) 1883.

[1] Danish translation, 1873.
[2] French translation, 1878.
[3] Italian translation, 1881, 1890.
[4] French translation (Bibliothèque Rose), 1884.
[5] Including the essay on "Romance and Realism."

Bibliography

Princess Napraxine. 3 vols. (Chatto and Windus.) 1884.

Othmar. 3 vols. (Chatto and Windus.) 1885.

A Rainy June.[1] (Maxwell.) [1885.]

Don Gesualdo. (Tillotson's Shilling Fiction, Routledge.) 1886.

A House Party. (Hurst and Blackett.) 1887.

Guilderoy. 3 vols. (Chatto and Windus.) 1889.

Ruffino and Other Stories. (Chatto and Windus.) 1890.

Syrlin. 3 vols. (Chatto and Windus.) 1890.

Santa Barbara and Other Tales. (Chatto and Windus.) 1891.

The Tower of Taddeo. 3 vols. (Heinemann.) 1892.

The New Priesthood: a Protest against Vivisection.[2] 1893.

Two Offenders and Other Tales. (Chatto and Windus.) 1894.

The Silver Christ and A Lemon Tree. (Unwin.) 1894.

Toxin. (Unwin.) 1895.

Views and Opinions. (Methuen.) 1895.

Le Selve and Other Tales. (Unwin.) 1896.

The Massarenes. (Sampson Low.) 1897.

Dogs. (Simpkin, Marshall.) 1897.

An Altruist. (Unwin.) 1897.

La Strega and Other Stories. (Sampson Low.) 1899.

The Waters of Edera. (Unwin.) 1900.

Critical Studies. (Unwin.) 1900.

Street Dust and Other Stories. (White and Bell.) 1901.

Helianthus. (Macmillan.) 1908.

[1] New edition, Unwin, 1901.
[2] A pamphlet.

INDEX

331

Index

Index

Index

Index

Index

UNWIN BROTHERS, LIMITED, THE GRESHAM PRESS, WOKING AND LONDON